The Chain Letter of the Soul

NEW AND SELECTED POEMS

Also by Bill Holm

Poetry

Playing the Black Piano

The Dead Get By with Everything

Boxelder Bug Variations

Prose

The Windows of Brimnes: An American in Iceland

The Heart Can Be Filled Anywhere on Earth

Faces of Christmas Past

Eccentric Islands: Travels Real and Imaginary

Coming Home Crazy: An Alphabet of China Essays

Landscape of Ghosts (with Bob Firth)

Chocolate Chip Cookies for Your Enemies

The Music of Failure

The Quiet Hours - Mike Melman, Bill Holm

The Chain Letter of the Soul

NEW AND SELECTED POEMS

Bill Holm

milkweed
editions

Published 2009 by Milkweed Editions
Printed in Canada
Cover design by Brad Norr
Cover photo by Jonathan Chapman
Interior design by Rachel Holscher, Bookmobile
The text of this book is set in Bembo.
10 11 12 13   5 4 3 2

First Edition

Please turn to the back of this book for a list of the
sustaining funders of Milkweed Editions.

Library of Congress Cataloging-in-Publication Data

Holm, Bill, 1943–2009
    The chain letter of the soul : new and selected poems /
by Bill Holm. — 1st ed.
        p.   cm.
    ISBN 978-57131-444-4 (pbk. : alk. paper)
    I. Title
    PS3558.O3558C47 2009
    811'.54—dc22
                                                2009021235

This book is printed on acid-free paper.

The Chain Letter of the Soul

Detached Retina

Mozart with Kathleen

Storm Coming to Seattle

II. BOXELDER BUG VARIATIONS

IV. PLAYING THE BLACK PIANO

For it is life we want. We want the world, the whole beautiful world, alive—and we alive in it. That is the actual god we long for and seek, yet we have already found it, if we open our senses, our whole bodies, thus our souls. That is why I have written and intend to continue until someone among you takes up the happy work of keeping the chain letter of the soul moving along into whatever future will come.

—Bill Holm

The Chain Letter of the Soul

I. New Poems

The Other Shoe

The Wisdom in a Rondo

In a rondo the same tune
sings again, again, again,
with something else between.
Why shouldn't your music
resemble your life? The same tune
come back in the same key?
You keep falling in love with the same
woman by different names, you take
the same job you never liked in the first place.
You buy the same house over and over,
on different streets, in different states.
The same toast, the same coffee.
Lead with the same foot in the same
dance, scratch the same itch with
the same finger. All in E major
or whatever key you start
until the last page when the double bar
signals you won't be hearing
that tune anymore. Unless
by chance the universe
loves repetition even more
than you and keeps the rondo circling,
searching for a new place to sing.

Ars Poetica

What are the poets trying to accomplish
with their chisels, brushes, quills, pencils,
ballpoints, felt-tips, something with a plug?
Write their names on the river?
Leave love notes in the clouds?
Confess their sins to the rain?
Find truth under the snow?
We fool ourselves, of course—
anything but eating, shitting, fucking,
or maybe hacking and hewing
is completely beside the point.
Shakespeare, Tao Chien, Homer, Pushkin,
Basho, Gilgamesh, Walt Whitman,
Anonymous—all wastes of time.
Your practical uncles were always right.
Still, if we move this word over here—
take out a line there—make it sing better—
there may be a surprise in it—though maybe not.
But we'll do it anyway, to pass,
as Buddha says, the time—
to thicken the plot. What else
have we got to do until the end?

Didgeridoo in Hofsós

Tom from Scotland with his didgeridoo
strides around the sitting room
playing Iceland out the window
into proper form. There's the mountain,
there's the boat, there the piled stones.
The windows vibrate in their frames
at the honking of this fundamental tone.
When he plays it in the road, the clouds
seem to arrange themselves in
parallelograms above the water.
Its one tone is all tones, a one-note
orchestra to serenade the universe.
Bloodwood, Tom says, from Australia,
pointing it at the sea as tide begins
retreating from the beach. The didgeridoo
is almost as tall as Tom
and ends in a cloven hoof.
His teacher in Scotland told him to play
the landscape as he moved over it.
Here's a score, he says; scratched sketches,
mispelled words, a walking song.

"Up the low green hill—past the field with the black stones in a
row—along the crooked creek—three pigeons on a clothesline—
two puddles in the street—one bramble bush—the broken windows
in the shed—one cloud overhead."

He honks his bloodwood tube again—
but now it seems a subtle sound,
full of nuance, evocation, texture,
Iceland growing a body before us,
never having existed until
the didgeridoo blows it to life
at the beginning of the world.

At the Farmer's Bank in Hofsós

Pálmi the banker likes poetry,
tells me who he reads: Jónas, K.N., Stefan G.,
asks me what I'm writing.
"Bad news for bankers, I'm afraid.
I'm writing poetry every day.
It won't put much in my account."
"Then you need a new pen," he says,
handing me the heavy silver model
reserved for good customers.
"Write plenty of poems with this."
He resumes adding his columns of kronur.
I don't tell him he's unusual because
he wouldn't believe it. I go home
and write a half-dozen poems. A poet
should never disappoint his banker.

Addict

No piano for a week.
My fingers find chords under
the covers in sleep.
A page of Beethoven clicks
onto the interior screen,
scrolls slowly toward
the next movement. Even if
your practical self licks
your addiction in daylight,
hands take over when eyelids fall
and the soul never gives up
a single addiction
no matter how white
your knuckles turn while
you feel around for music.

I Began the Day in My Sixty-fifth Year

I began the first day in the new year, my sixty-fifth, by having a long conversation with myself—aloud and alone. In a wired house, I suppose the paddy wagon would arrive soon to take me off to where I could be made, with drugs and counseling, better suited for capitalism and American life. But I'm safe; my house is old, ramshackle and unwinnable. So I babble away to myself, always in crisp, parsable sentences, adorned with the sizable word hoard I've filed away from reading these thousands of books for well over a half century. I ask myself questions that nobody else has bothered to ask—though they are, I'm convinced, the only important questions. Then I answer myself firmly, wisely, and (I hope) with wit, clean thinking, and no trace of indulgent senti-ment. I address myself always formally by name, for fear there's some interloper inside, waiting to fool me. I give myself orders— for work, action, behavior, generally the only orders I bother to follow. If you want to know what I am *really* like, at bottom, what I think—of you, god, or the state of the world—arrange to hide (very discreetly so early in the morning) and listen. It's my own Song of Myself, and I will tell you more than Walt Whitman ever did (though not, I'm afraid, so lyrically).

Where does this voice come from? Is there more than one? No, I'm afraid it's my ordinary voice, the one I use to actually speak to you, or to a thousand people in a room, though now the diction and content are untailored to a particular audience. It's the voice I had from birth, and used even in the '40s to inter-rogate myself in my own bedroom when I was sure my parents were far away, otherwise occupied and couldn't hear a word of it. What would they have thought of such internal dramas—rather, dialogues—going on in the childish voice of their treasured son? Or maybe they knew and had such conversations in solitude themselves. Maybe we all do—we owners of consciousness.

This is no soliloquy, but a continual interruption—often saying No or Don't Be Silly to myself when such measures of verbal negation are called for. It must be aloud; mental dialogue is too easily shaped by longing and practicality. This voice requires currents of air to resist and carry it, to be present in the concrete world. Maybe it's a form of internal music being composed by an improviser as great as Beethoven was said to be—Beethoven who, though stone deaf, howled and raged and babbled to himself while he entered into conversation with the patterns of notes banging their way into his brain. Maybe this voice explains why humans even make works of art, rather than sensibly dying with them still inside.

January 2, 2009

Untitled

After seventeen years of circling,
waiting for the other shoe to drop,
we decided to give up and marry—
and on a cold, sunny Sunday
in an empty rural courthouse, we did.
The guests were all throwing up from flu,
so we ate the nuptial rhubarb pie alone,
wondering if this was the other shoe.
Now three years after, still under icy sun,
we're keeping our ears alert
for any sudden thumps in undusted corners.
So far, so good. We have now
both loved and endured each other
a long time. Let's raise a glass to ourselves:
while the world was careening madly forward,
we parked our souls in the shade of the chaos,
and here we are, still alive, and pie
or no pie, still capable of joy.

January 22, 2009

The Miniaturization of the World

Earbud

Earbud—a tiny marble sheathed in foam
to wear like an interior earring so you
can enjoy private noises wherever you go,
protected from any sudden silence.
Only check your batteries, then copy
a thousand secret songs and stories
on the tiny pod you carry in your pocket.
You are safe now from noises made
by other people, other machines, by chance,
noises you have not chosen as your own.
To get your attention, I touch your arm
to show you the tornado or the polar bear.
Sometimes I catch you humming or talking to the air
as if to a shrunken lover waiting in your ear.

The Industrial Revolution Comes to Iceland at Last

I ask how many in Húsavík think
the proposed aluminum smelter a few miles
outside this lovely and civilized town,
almost on the Arctic Circle,
a bad idea. Siggi says, "Two—but one,"
a schoolteacher, "moved back to Reykjavík."
I wait. "Now there's me. Maybe a few more
who don't dare speak." Far south of here
the big glacier feeds the river Skjálfandi
which feeds the bay fresh water
which feeds the multitude of whales
who entertain the tourists for a fee.
We can't stand in the way of Progress:
jobs, prosperity, the future, reality.
That would be unrealistic, unpatriotic,
furthermore financially unsound.
Meanwhile the Future stands prepared
to knock us over with his bulldozer,
spit out our bones and drown our meat
in the new electric lagoon he's digging.
Progress, a rabid mink the size of a wolf,
means to bite us in the throat to shut us up,
until we can all enjoy together
dining on his smoking droppings.

Hardfish

I spent a morning helping Viggó the hardfish man fill out—in
English—the Shengen visa application papers. Numbers, num-
bers, numbers, check boxes here and here, permission required
to prove you are a human being and not a bacillus or a plot
against the state and the economy. Finally done, three pages,
sign here. Evgenia from Tashkent, Uzbekistan, requests permis-
sion to spend three months in Hofsós, Skagafjörð, North Iceland
to work and learn the hardfish business. In Tashkent, fish rots in
the market at its steady hundred degrees, no freezer, no elec-
tricity. Hardfish, dried and jerked til it is impervious to heat—or
some say to teeth—could be a market there, thinks Viggó. So the
Uzbek Evgenia requests to come halfway across the planet, enter
the province of the rich. Viggó SMSes (whatever that is . . .)
Tashkent for the address and number of Evgenia's previous em-
ployer. Back it comes in a few minutes. Another blank filled. It
doesn't take long these days to hear from Tashkent. Imagine a
letter mailed one hundred years ago, in 1907. The long desert,
the Siberian taiga, the Caucasus, the Baltic bogs, the ship heav-
ing through the north Atlantic, the wooden postbox strapped to
the horse's back in Reykjavík for the long ride north. Maybe six
months instead of six minutes. Maybe we all lived longer then,
and could afford the time. What language do we use to pass mes-
sages back and forth from Tashkent to Hofsós? Uzbek? Icelandic?
Better we write in Latin or Arabic, or old Chinese, the languages
of scholars' worldly discourse. But this is 2007, and cyberspace
is humming with English. The linchpin between those worlds
is hardfish, which looked and tasted much the same a century
ago. For all I know, some has lasted for the whole century, if no-
body ate it all during hard times. Viggó thanks me with an arm-
load of his plastic-sealed hardfish (haddock and cod), and a bottle
of vodka to wash it down. He's taking Evgenia's Shengen papers
to a bureaucrat's office in Reykjavík to be stamped. He hopes for
the best: she looks a promising employee—to maybe spread the
gospel of hardfish in central Asia. I wish him good luck on the
trip. Tonight I'll find a tub of butter for the hardfish and a glass
for the vodka. No one will sound the call to prayer in Hofsós to
interrupt me in my pleasure.

Typhoid Albert

Someone who never heard of Australia
brought a pair of rabbits to Iceland.
To amuse the children, he said.
Unfortunately not gay rabbits,
they did what rabbits do best:
hatched a rabble of themselves
and began to dine on Iceland.
This same benefactor
brought venomous snakes
to Guam and Hawaii,
brought fox to Tasmania
where they eat their fill
of five or six soon-extinct
species you've never heard of.
What will Typhoid Albert bring
to my house in Minneota?
Malarial mosquitoes? Poisonous spiders?
Or is he content to have brought
lampreys to Lake Superior
where they suck out the guts
of mild-mannered local fish?
What's to be learned from Typhoid Albert?
Travel to new places naked.
Leave your opinions and your pets at home.
On this planet, neither everything
nor everyone belongs everywhere
even if they have money to get there.

American Speech

After six weeks without meeting an American
or hearing English spoken by our voices,
I overhear a television show at Hallgrímur's house.
I'm staring out the window at the sea, my back to the picture.
Brynhildur, twelve, watches with full attention,
reading the Icelandic sliding over the bottom of the screen.
Awesome! someone says. I'll always be there for you.
You're really special. Awesome rings through again.
Flat vowels, bright singsong, no clauses at all,
only a few words. My god, is that my own voice I hear?
What do I expect Americans to say to each other?
Invade Iraq? Kill a queer for Christ? I'll have another
helping of money, please? Find me a buffalo to shoot?
I fix full attention on the sea, listen close to its murmuring.

Fourth of July Speech, 2007

It's America's 231st birthday,
and here I am, the real thing,
three thousand-odd miles away from its shores.
Two hundred ninety-seven kilometers north of my embassy
where now at 4:15 a reception
celebrating this birthday is underway.
I sent regrets. Instead I took a nap,
did not enjoy patriotic dreams.
Am I lonesome for the homeland
secured or endangered? No.
Do I miss? Please check choices:
Food? No. Pizza has triumphed.
English? Plenty of it, and better quality here.
News? A relief to have none of it.
Weather? Ye gods, I'm from Minnesota!
Landscape? Ditto, of course.
Freedom? Don't begin the battle of clichés.
Too many dead from that old canard.
The dollar? Sixty kronur buys one today.
Euros? Pounds? Yen? Don't ask.
Friends? Some there, some here,
some in other places.
We will get around to each other wherever.
Family? Yes, but all dead, all there.
Missing the dead does not require your presence.
It can be done anywhere.
I miss cheap gas and cheap whiskey,
here *bensín* and *áfengi*.
Call it whatever you want,
nine dollars a gallon or ninety dollars a quart:
too damn dear a price.
I miss Walt Whitman and Henry Thoreau,
Mark Twain and Charles Ives,
Scott Joplin and Jelly Roll Morton.
But them I carry with me always
wherever I am, in a private bag

airport security cannot find.
Finally, I miss one woman
who would be here if she could
but for American necessities,
and will be after a while, or
I will be there, driving around
on the cheap, enjoying a cheap drink.
But for now, my head bounces
back and forth like a big tennis ball
on a court six time zones wide.

Patriotism

When the shadow of my country crosses my mind,
It is not flag I see or anthem I hear
Nor the president's head on a post-office wall
Nor a foreign policy only an idiot could stomach.
If those are my country, find me another.
But I see faces, mostly dead now,
Hear voices, mostly not in English,
See the boxelder tree out my bedroom window,
A dark green sky before a tornado,
A blizzard so big we tunneled under it,
Hear slow, out-of-tune hymns at the funeral
Of an old lady born in the nineteenth century.
The FBI has never heard of my country.

Cell Phone Sequence

I

Each has its own song, only two bars long,
which it plays over and over and over,
never arriving at the third bar.
Some play *Eine Kleine Nachtmusik.*
Some play "Turkey in the Straw."
Some play "Over the Rainbow" or "Hey Jude."
Mine honks like a car horn, or a goose on steroids,
or even—like a phone.

II

It tells precise time wherever you are.
It changes time zones before you think to look.
How does it know where your trips take you?
Or when you return? Do the secret police
man a surveillance station inside your mobile?
It will also take photographs, play games,
send cryptic messages by thumb, talk back to you
if you are ever alone and in need of human noise.
I know how to do none of this—by special request.
Don't even show me how! How do I make a phone call?
Feed in the number, scroll, then auto dial.
Different from ringing Central, probably Betty or Hazel,
telling her the number you want, checking news and weather,
then waiting forty-five minutes for a line to clear,
until at last you hear two shorts and a long.
No Mozart or Beatles for another fifty years.

III

The cell phone honks in my pocket.
It is small, oddly heavy, covers half my palm,
shaped like a miniature coffin, gunmetal gray steel.
A name: NOKIA. Is little Nokia embalmed inside?

Am I Nokia's personal pallbearer?
There's an inch-square window at one end
that lights up pale blue when I touch it.
Will Nokia's dead face peer back at me from inside the glass?
Is that Nokia's honking tickling my nipple?
Does Nokia wish like Jesus to rise from the dead?
The power of his honking vibrates the coffin,
but I'm afraid it will take a clever angel
to roll that lid away and let him out.

IV

Last night, Nokia rang me with news
from halfway across the planet, news so terrible,
so full of black grief that I wished to pulverize
Nokia, like Cassandra, for the bringing of it.
The size of the black stone inside this news
required an orchestra of sad trombones and cellos,
or an organ the size of Devil's Tower, or the mournful
howling of a hundred thousand wolves,
or maybe only a simple human voice,
speaking not through an iron coffin, but in this room,
a human with skin and hair to touch, to prove
that something is alive, that we can weep together
at news so black that weeping cannot lift it.

August 2, 2007: American News

More black news from Minnesota.
A bridge over the Mississippi falls: nine dead, twenty missing,
    details unclear . . .
All this arrives in half-understood Icelandic over the car radio
    while driving to Akureyri.
I imagine cars hurtling over the interstate bridge into the
    now-tepid waters of the river.
The sky above a humid hundred, cries and shrieks muffled in
    the saturated air.

Bridges are not supposed to fall in invincible, "can-do" America.
The Brooklyn Bridge does not fall.
The iron gates of the locks in the Panama Canal have opened
    and closed every day since 1913.
The generators hum below the Hoover Dam to feed the electrical
    jolt that cools, lights, and irrigates the west.
The motor in the old Buick purrs after 250,000 miles.
We build to last! We are the world's engineers!

Suddenly we lose all our steadily stupider wars; the currency
    evaporates; we're afraid of every moving shadow.
The FedEx clerk in Minneapolis has never heard of Iceland.
That in Europe? We don't deliver there. Where's Retchivelt?
The codebook lies on the table in front of him: number 286.
But he either can't or won't read it.
So goes business—as Charles Wilson said: the business of America.

Three-quarters of us believe in a personal god who saves and
    punishes.
Three-quarters of us can't find Canada, France, or the Pacific
    on a map.
We believe in one true god, but not in geography.
Every day Paris Hilton and Lindsay Lohan appear in the Reykjavík
    newspapers: what are they up to now?
Tomorrow I suppose it will be pictures of cars dropping off a
    collapsed bridge,

down into the Father of Waters that divides us, east from west,
the waters that begin in Scandinavian, safe, efficient Minnesota
    and now will carry bodies downstream in the current
    through twenty-seven locks and dams that may or may not
    open and close and open again as they are directed
    so that the ghosts can make their way toward whatever is left
    of New Orleans.

Oh United States! Walt Whitman thought you might wake up—
    though he was not sure—and he wept for you.
Your sleep is deeper now than ever before, and none of your
    "information systems" are worth a damn to wake you, to hold
    up the girders of whatever bridge might carry you through
    even one more century of history.

Hard Money—Two Views

I

I find on my window ledge
a dropped coin from home, a gold dollar.
On one side, an Indian head
made up by a committee.
On the obverse, a flying eagle,
wings spread, on its way to chew
into something dead.
A carrion eater
and an artificial mother.
This dollar says it trusts God,
but don't take the coin as proof.
Gold is only the color. Still,
the dollar is always the dollar
with whatever head it wears.

II

On the kronur coin, a cod, a fish
so insignificant
that Icelanders refuse to eat it.
Then it's fish after fish all the way up
to the hundred—a lumpsucker,
a primitive and ugly creature
valued only for roe.
No human head is here
important enough to become
money, until we reach paper,
which burns, and disappears into the wind.

Christian TV in Reykjavík

After a day of privacy in Reykjavík,
I turn on the TV for company.
First surf: Icelandic news with a long face.
Second surf: Euro Cup soccer match,
Slovenia and somebody.
Third and last possible surf: Omega,
a parade of saviors
with southern accents in English, just for me!
First famous Jimmy Swaggart,
his now-bloated face
announcing that he needs
more money to do God's work.
Then a commanding woman, Joyce Meyer,
tight brown curls, pink dress,
a first-class word slinger
who strides back and forth on stage,
jabbing at her Bible to drive her point.
They demand I buy
whatever it is they are selling:
salvation by the gallon,
a low-mileage soul, a sleeping berth
in the Pullman car to Jesus.
Somewhere north, an old mountain farmer watches
without a word of English.
He sees the face of the door-to-door drummer
coming with sample cases crammed:
waterless cookware, encyclopedias,
vegetable shredders, vitamin cures,
whatever you don't want, don't need,
can't afford, have to be frightened
by the prospect of not buying,
of missing the final miracle
that will make your life right
and heal your sheep of scabies.

A hell of a deal in Icelandic, too.
Here is one American gift
to the whole world: God for sale,
along with a nice selection of merchandise.

Transfigured Phone

On his way underwater
to rescue a dropped tub of cod,
Þórhallur forgets the cell phone still
tucked in his pocket. Now
it is a sea phone, damp and salted,
gets satellite signals from a mile down,
sad songs from lonesome whales,
phone sex with mermaids,
911s from the soon-to-drown,
too late to save them now.

Motherless Lamb

Sometimes, for sheep reasons unknowable to humans, a ewe scorns her new lamb. If this were sheep opera, she would sing "Noli Me Tangere" and the violins would sigh. But on an Iceland farm, the lamb comes into the house where it is fed by hand, so Dídí, the lovely blonde farmer's daughter who cooks in the village, turns temporary mama. The lamb, half pet, half baby, follows her into the café's kitchen where she is frying cod. It wanders from table to table, nuzzling the customers' feet, as if begging for alms. "Oh, for cute!" says one American customer.

Later, I stop at Dídí's house on an errand and find her on her leather couch with Dúi, her man, the lamb snuggled in between them, watching "American Idol" so many light-years removed from this pastoral scene. "So you two have started another family," I smirk. The lamb bleats. Maybe it's milk time. I scratch its soft white ears. Soon you will grow up, my little lamb chop, to discover the world where we are all, one way or another, hypothetical lamb chops. Meanwhile, there are worse pastimes to cultivate than artificial mothering. We'll all need a bit of that at the beginning and at the end.

Hypothetical Polar Bear

Rumors of the third white bear in June
arrived where he is never supposed to be—
on Skagi, a bleak thumb of bog and lake
stuck into the cold sea north of Iceland,
home only for farmers, trout, and sheep.
It's summer, so he alone is white
in this bare and treeless place.
Imagine him swimming from so far away,
his heavy body padding over the heath,
wondering what here is fit to eat.
Not our sheep. Not our children. Not our wives.
We've already shot the first-arriving two,
so whenever the shot comes right again,
whether you exist or not, we'll shoot you.

Steinbítur

A man comes from the sea into the parking lot in front of the restaurant. He's still dressed in boots and slicker, carrying a wet, gray-green fish about two feet long. He holds the fish by the tail, head down. It's an odd shape, a long, fat rectangle more like a club or a bat than a fish. A half dozen American ladies notice the fish. "What is it?" asks one. "*Steinbítur,* stone biter, an ocean wolffish." They've neither heard of it nor seen one. It seems unfishlike to them. "Very big, strong teeth," says the man. One woman touches the head, as if she were going to pet the fish. She shrieks, pulls her hand back, looks for blood. "Even dead, they bite," the man says. "It's what they do, all they know. They bite stones, after all."

The grayish-green skin is cured like leather, tough and beautiful for purses and bags. The woman holds her slightly wounded hand tight, as if it might escape and slap the fish. She is already imagining the Opera Ball next year, the admiring comments on her new clutch bag: "Skin of a stone biter," she says. "From Iceland. Big, strong teeth."

News in Reverse Gear: Yesterday's *Fréttablaðið*

At the Hofsós village store,
news arrives a day late:
yesterday's weather, yesterday's kronur rate.
Sometimes travelers bring papers
with week-old news in English, and
I read them all backward, begin
on the eighteenth, proceed to the eighth.
History now unhappens day by day.
Humans get their second chance to dodge
catastrophe. Thank god
we didn't invade Iraq or build the dam!
We missed whatever splattered on our heads.
If I buy kronur, sell dollars yesterday,
I'll be rich tomorrow! To celebrate,
I invite you to a garden party last night
just before the onslaught of big rain
and the hurricane winds arrived.

The Miniaturization of the World

In Papua, New Guinea, or the Amazon jungle, our Stone-Age cousins shrink the heads of their vanquished enemies, to make small whatever they fear. If you were clever enough, you could make them almost disappear. Now fist-size, the right formula might shrink them down further to thumbnail-size. That would satisfy your interior rage, a hollow gourd with a whole village inside that could never trouble you again. On sleepless nights your children could shake the thumb-head rattle for hours to calm you through the long night.

Your new iPod weighs hardly over an ounce, half the size of a playing card, thin and trim. It holds one hundred fifty hours of tunes, all your favorites: Schubert, Leadbelly, Springsteen, Copland, Prince, the Rolling Stones, the Grateful Dead, Handel's *Messiah*. Just insert your soft earbud to enjoy this tiny box of shrunken music on your own long nights.

Winter Facts

The first fact on January third
is the fact of winter,
more than dead banks, lost wars,
violence erupting here and there.
The fundamental fact is snow.
Is the glacier coming or going?
One man who loves the Weather Channel
watches the whole electronic map
swallowed up by snow
bite by bite until it's white
with fallen snow on snow,
as the old hymn says,
and this first fact of winter
plants its icy boots on us.
Not forever, but long enough
to make us think.

Spiritual Economy

Like Christians, Jews, and Muslims,
I believe in one true god who is
my father, Big Bill, me his only son,
and all the ghost tribes you can imagine,
some holy, mostly otherwise.
What's my proof? There: that stone;
the loaf of bread; the crow's feathers;
that road splotch of mashed raccoon;
you, should you happen to appear.
I hear god's voice in the "Pastoral Sonata,"
sounding the low-D thump that starts it,
in the crow's cackle, the soft snoring in my head,
the old lady's hummed Alzheimer's tune.
Doesn't everyone believe all of this?
Why should I differ from my fellow humans?
I don't put on the dog, or claim a revelation.
But I do not believe in the economy
even though it claims to have collapsed.
To collapse is to have once existed,
but I've never heard sufficient proof of that.
To participate in IS you must once have BEEN.
No one denies stone, crow, bread,
or fails to hear the D, the cackles, snoring, tune.
But put a trillion on your kitchen table:
piles of millions, certificates of billions,
bundles of derivative credit default swaps.
Still got room for a coffee cup or two?
Light it with a match, watch it disappear.
Whose name was written on it? Mine? Yours?
We need to know to notify the next of kin.
Thus did worldly goods pass back and forth,
from hand to hand. They will go on passing:
the daily procession of the body parts of god.

Mozart Sale

The mail brings news of "Awesome value!"
"The complete works of Mozart!"
"170 CDs for $129.99!"
"Less than 80 cents a CD!"
"Free shipping while supplies last!"
Now at last we can tally
Mozart's value to the last cent,
corner the Mozart futures market,
but only while supplies last.
After all, no new Mozart since 1791.
The universe owns all the Mozart
it will ever get. Trust the market
always rising on scarce goods of awesome
quality. Never have humans
needed Mozart more than this day.
Such a price for all of him!
Complete, achieved, boxed and wrapped!
Put in your earbud—play them all
one after the other: concertos, operas,
masses, sonatas, quartets, serenades,
one hundred seventy hours of awesome value,
a week and a day of your life,
wired into this electric crypt
with surround-sound Mozart.
When you unbud your ears, you might
be a different sort of human, but
on the other hand, you might not.
Is that Mozart's fault? What do you expect
for one hundred thirty bucks? The voice of Yahweh
roaring in a whirlwind?

Senior Crime Wave in Japan

Maybe to restore Samurai honor
Japanese geezers and crones
take to armed robbery, purse snatching,
shoplifting, not gold or diamonds
but fruit, fish, and vegetables.
Since they make slow getaways
with their crutches, canes, bent backs,
they are usually caught and jailed.
"Nice and warm here, soft bed, plenty of food,"
says one eighty-year-old jailbird.
A peculiar crime wave here where
the old are revered for their wisdom.
Poverty? Wrinkles? Loneliness? Pain?
Where's that noble stoicism
we all counted on them for?
Even your sainted grandmother
means to disconnect you from
the sentimental idiocy of myth.
The old need whatever you own
and more. They'll get it
one way if not another.

Snow Birds

A month below zero now, we remind each other.
Twenty straight days of snow.
Up in the Cities, the car exhaust froze on the highway.
At rush hour. Made rust and black ice.
Five hundred accidents just in the morning.
Ninety-three, had plenty of money, didn't pay the gas bill.
The company turned off his heat. Froze to death
inside his house, wearing four layers.
Did it serve him right, we ask each other?
And just what does right service mean
in the middle of the annual assault on
human nature?
The Russians have used this mercy for centuries
to save themselves from the likes of Napoleon and Hitler.
What use do we intend to make of it?
It won't save our soul, or our sanity, or even our money.
All those things shall leak away and diminish
under the bludgeonings of its icy rays—
the old shall fall and crack, the intemperate
young shall grow proud flesh, the rest will burrow
down into themselves to try to outlast it.
Most of them will—a little paler, a little sadder,
counting how many times this will happen before the end.
But I will not burrow. I will leave, go
where I sit now in this desert garden in the sun,
remembering everything that I have left,
whatever I was too cold to love, wrapped in
my afghan of self pity and claustrophobia.
I was a coward and proud of it. Fuck you.

February 3, 2009

Super Bowl Chamber Music

Mozart and Haydn quartets on a Sunday afternoon,
Free! at the cement-block Lutheran church,
hedged around with palms, mesquite, saguaros.
In the rest of America, fans gather for the Super Bowl,
the biggest audience in human history,
assembled in a million houses to howl and cheer,
to nibble nachos, little snacks, guacamole,
to go for the gusto, to teach America to sing,
for this is what we love, more than Mozart and Haydn.
But a respectable room of listeners have gathered,
mostly old, gray Scandinavian ghosts listening
in alert silence for Mozart trying to find his way to C Major,
for Haydn pretending he's at an outdoor vaudeville
making frenzied music for jugglers and sleight-of-hand quick-
    change artists.
Maybe this is really the right music for football,
the pigskin spiraling through the air between two violins,
the quarterback giving the signal to the cello
before he falls back to fake a long pass to the viola.
Maybe it's all one event after all when you listen
from halfway up the craggy mountain out the window.

Untitled

In the north with its long frost and bluster,
in the frozen houses even of the rich,
some Sven or Gretchen kept awake all night
to keep feeding the fire new mouthfuls
of coal or cobs or peat or split wood
so cold could not come all the way indoors
to freeze you in your sleep. The Lord and Lady
did not arise from their tapestried beds
to feed anything at all, much less a fire.
So who, I ask, kept the kingdom running?
With no fire, there is only chaos or death,
but if the fire must be rekindled daily
ten times from scratch, there is only waiting,
the border undefended, the taxes uncollected,
the full chamber pots frozen solid til spring.
And who will carry the buckets of spent ash
out to be dumped in the snow? Even the final ash. The ash?

February 12, 2009

Untitled

A cistern of dead language
drains out from the newspapers and radios
every morning now for months:
mortgage credit foreclosure stimulus
jumpstart consumer bailout package.
No one has any idea what any of it means,
much less the stentorian verses that proclaim it.
It is a serenade for the winter wind to play,
performed and sung by a company of the deaf and dumb.
All the ordinary citizen sees are puddles
of soggy mash, money leaked out of every pore,
pale green, half-fermented, squishy underfoot.
It neither feels nor smells good, nor sane, nor logical,
so all the language about it, breathed by the artificial wise,
is only a river of corpse words, unconnected
to whatever is alive in the actual world.

February 19, 2009

Untitled

New graves this year in the Patagonia hilltop graveyard. Here
gringo and latino lie down together, as if no chasm ever kept
them apart, the solidarity of the dead, all molding and decom-
posing into the unison dust of earth. Here, new pink and violet
plastic garlands, Xmas lights, a toy motorcycle, must be Lopez;
there, a square gray stone: F. Newton and a pair of dates, could be
New England. Here they can wave daily, greet each others' wraiths,
as indeed they might have done in life. This small, brushy hilltop
is ringed by a fifty-mile radius of craggy mountains, steep arroyos,
desert grass, and scrub brush, here the center of everything, the
omphalos of the universe. Overhead the Milky Way circles nightly,
Venus keeps her red light in the western window. You may as well
die and go under here at the center of galaxies. You spend quite
enough of your life standing by the side door, ignored, beside the
point. Here you become the point itself. Too bad you're dead for it.

February 20, 2009

Detached Retina

Remembrance of Things Past

You taught me English once, she says,
now almost thirty years ago.
Impossible! You are a wrinkled owl,
not some blonde and gossamer hummingbird.
So many years . . . What did I say?
What grand poems do you remember?
A few lines of Walt Whitman maybe?
Only that you once got very drunk at a party,
danced wildly, and fell downstairs.
I, on the other hand, remember nothing at all,
neither your name, your face, nor anything you said.
What, she asks, have you been doing these thirty years?
Not much of anything. I haven't even been
drunk a single time, but meeting you now inspires me
to think of hoisting the bottle up again.

Detached Retina

The gray shade drops over the eye—
as if darkening one bedroom window for the night.
You wake with half the world amputated:
day in the left, night in the right.

———

Maybe a man could buy an eye patch,
start to sell shirts for a living—
or invest in half a Seeing-Eye dog.
Waiting like Puddinhead to kill the other half—
or console himself with the often-told lie
that half a life is better than no life at all.

———

Maybe owning two of almost everything
is nature's fail-safe: two eyes, ears, nostrils,
kidneys, lungs, testicles, hands, feet.
One goes to hell—you're still in the ball game.
But only one of the big machinery:
brain, heart, penis, liver. Blow those and you're out.

———

You hear stories of the one-eyed—
how it seems to concentrate the powers:
Creeley, Harrison, my Minneota buddy Borson.
Maybe there *is* a consolation prize.

———

After all, god himself by another name
arrives on his eight-legged horse, one eye gone,
two ravens waiting on his shoulder
to snatch out the other,
should they catch him lying just once more.

———

But medical science has broken the Maginot Line,
advancing its heavy armor against the thieves of time.
There is an operation, a strategy, a master plan:
slice open the eyeball, drain the vitreous juice.
Into the empty sac, insert a bubble of gas.
Nail the retina back where it belongs with a laser gun.
Hang down your head for weeks. Gravity and new juice
dissolve the bubble. As it dies, light barges back in.
The world is whole but fuzzy, as if painted by Van Gogh.

———

Nothing is ever quite fixed as good as new;
every fender bender to the body leaves a dent
that never can be quite painted over or pounded out.
Still all the parts go on working after their fashion.
A lot of miles left in the old wreck and cheap to boot.

———

Tolstoy imagines Ivan Ilych entering at the end
a world of pure white light as the real one goes black.
Both eyes down for the count for good.
Two retinas detached and not a laser gun in sight,
the brain, heart, penis, liver giving up at last.
If you are forced to bet, put your money on the dark.

Lóa

It never occurs to the plover that
her black summer breast is beautiful.
She was born to it, will die with it,
is neither proud nor ashamed of it.
She ambles through wet grass behind the school,
her mind and her attention given
entirely to worms, the new crop hatched
and waiting after the spring rain.
She doesn't know her melancholy hooting
is lovely, the alto clarinet of birds.
Even her name in Iceland, *Lóa,*
is melodious, but she won't answer to it.

Pink Girl and Cows

Thirty or forty reddish-brown cows, milk bags heavy and swinging, clump down the dirt road to their driveway, their barn, their relief. A little blonde girl in a pink track suit, maybe eight years old, and two perky black-and-white dogs herd them home, keep them moving. There's no rushing this gang: clump, clump, clump. The little girl holds a switch but doesn't have to use it. She just keeps an eye out for stragglers. One of the dogs settles into the ditch for a quick nap. Not a grown-up in sight, just pink girl, dogs, red cows, the noise of birds: plovers, whimbrels, a pair of snipes cutting up the sky with buzz-saw wings.

And all around the girl and cows, an Icelandic meadow in full bloom on this early July afternoon, an almost symmetrically arranged parellelogram of purple lupine, yellow buttercups, white cotton grass, against a canvas of two-tone green: pale cut hay field, dark intense shaggy grass, over it the ice blue arctic sky, sun to the north, there in the distance the sea—still blue glass stretching north to the polar circle, then after a while the polar ice.

The pink girl and her slow cows stop traffic for ten minutes: one car, us. They round the bend to the farm. The still-awake dog sniffs the tires. That little girl, whatever her name—Guðrún, Helga, Jónína—might remember this afternoon with cows until 2087, maybe longer; Icelandic women last a long time. She will not remember the stopped car with the two middle-aged men in the front seat. Will she remember the switch of command in her hand, herding those tons of heavy-hooved, milk-swollen cows to their duty? Or remember the smell of the cut hay, colors of the flowers in the meadow, the sea a mile or two away, stretching everywhere you might want to go?

But why go anywhere else, when you already own this afternoon?

Spinoza's Bed

When Bento, Baruch Benedict, the blessed boy
Retired behind the velvet curtains that enclosed
The elegant old four-poster bed, his only patrimony,
What thoughts went through his drowsing head that they
Who knew him best found beautiful but those
Who knew him not at all called diabolical?
Did he mull over "those events of ordinary life"
He found empty and futile, neither good nor bad,
Except that "we are moved by them toward knowledge
Of the union of the mind with the whole of Nature"?
That he called God, because he thought that god enough.
After they finished damning him, the Jews cast him out.
The Christians did not want him, the Muslims were not asked.
He moved his bed upstairs in a modest workman's house,
Ground lenses for microscopes that would reveal
Inward secrets of the universe he called God,
Scribbled thoughtful letters all over Europe to any
He found rational enough to hear and think,
Always laboring over his laborious book of Ethics,
Made so difficult that only a few could read,
For if many understood, they'd kill him in a flicker.
He lived a cautious, courteous, quiet life,
Grinding his glass by day, talk and a pipe by night,
Then sleep in the same bed where his parents both
Conceived and birthed him, where he would die of dust.
He left little: a few books, shirts, mug and bowl, the bed.
From another angle, he left all the best a man can leave:
His thought, wisdom that might make us free and sane.
He was blessèd by name in all his languages
And so his work blesses us; for that we owe him praise.
He gave us the only God we will ever have.

Book Review: *Abandoned Farms,* Nökkvi Elíasson

In Húsavík I buy a picture book of abandoned farms:
concrete blackened, rotted, crumbling,
the interiors charnel houses for flies and bird bones.
What beauty is there in this that an aging man
on a sunny day would spend forty dollars on such a book
in some tourist shop and think it a great pleasure?
The steep concrete stairs once leading up to
the empty kitchen with rusted stove and broken table
cracked and fallen now. No easy way inside
to answer the ghostly call for coffee and *kleinur.*
Murky clouds lower over these scenes,
or a riled sea, or a gray snowdrift, a half-dead tree.
Behind these empty shells a field
of black stones, or lumpy hummocks of dried grass.
These pictures are all black-and-white. Did the color, once
alive in them, leach out over a century?
They remind their new owner of himself. He grows
black-and-white, too, ever faster now.

Hypnotism in Brimnes

This window watching—
maybe the mountain
and the light and the sea
hypnotized me.
You're falling back . . . back . . . back . . .
you cannot lift your feet
or arms at all. Just keep
eyes forward. Where are you now?
Here, in front of the window.
The coffee's grown cold, like the room.
But I cannot move.
Is anyone with you? No. Alone.
How old are you now?
A day younger than I will be tomorrow.
And where will you be tomorrow?
Gone maybe. Away from the window.
The light, the mountain, the sea.
Back . . . back . . . back . . . in a circle.
I write the same sentence over and over,
but never quite hear what it's saying.
Maybe if I snapped my fingers.

August 13, 2007

The Dig at Hólar

Jam your spade into the ground,
hoping for night crawlers maybe
or a good home for potatoes.
You have dug up history whether
you want it or not. Now—
play archeologist.
Handle this mud tenderly—
slow work with a fine brush.
You will find leavings in it
from the long parade of corpses
who have fertilized you.
That chunk of misshaped lead
comes from the alphabet, type
from the book you haven't read
that answered all your questions.
That pottery shard was once
part of the cup in which
your Ur-mother poured her tea.
That rusted metal thimble
with a broken handle once snuffed
candles by a beautiful woman's bed.
She is still waiting for you
after all these centuries,
and night crawlers live there, too.

Why I Hate the Turf Houses of My Ancestors: Tourist Reminders of "Ye Olde Iceland!"

The door says: Bow your head.
When you stand up, remember to bend.
Stand straight and you'll get a whack—
Don't think yourself too big
for your house; something inside you is
the right size for cramped quarters.
Get used to the dark. Light is a luxury.
Feel the wall: it's damp, musty earth.
Your grave will feel like this. Grass
will grow on its roof, too.
Smell that piss pot. Smell all twenty of them.
Enough shit there to fertilize a snowdrift.
The fish hanging in the next room gets
older and riper every day. That barrel
of sour whey holds seal fingers, blood pudding, testicles.
Don't worry. They will all arrive on your table
in good time. No other air til spring
will come to trade places with this air.
Cow, horse, even sheep live only a few
yards away, either below or alongside.
Be grateful for their heat, if not their stink.
There's your bed, a small, half-enclosed box,
a foot less of bed than of you.
Curl up. You will soon have company,
but only feet to kiss goodnight: the head
next to your feet will snore, cough up
phlegm, share its head lice with the quilt.
In this room, in the company of many others,
you will write great books, the glory of Europe,
translate Milton, tell ghost stories, record history.
You will even manage to father children,
sometimes with a wife, sometimes a housemaid,
sometimes, probably, with a ghost.
How you did it in this foul hovel
is a mystery to me who came from you,

not so long ago. If I had lived here,
I would have dreamed of killing them all,
then destroying the house with fire and axe,
but probably would only have killed myself,
hoping at least that the afterlife
would not be much like this, that eternity
required better quarters, more air and light.

Fried Chicken in Iceland

As if by magic incantation,
first-rate fried chicken legs
appear on the table in Brimnes—
greaseless, juicy, perfect.
What are the spices? asks Nelson,
gnawing on his fourth leg.
He is a gourmand, a connoisseur of wine.
Flour, salt, and pepper, says Donna from Illinois.
Everyone giggles, but keeps eating.
She does not add: knowing what you are doing
because of having done it before
a thousand times til frying anything
turns into breathing. In this regard,
it's a lot like playing music.
Keep practicing until it lives inside you;
then it will seem foolishly easy
to the unpracticed. Everything
is simple if you know how it's done.
That's why dying will come
so hard for everyone.

Hólar Concert

This eighteenth-century red stone cathedral,
smaller than a millionaire's parlor
or the lobby of a Holiday Inn,
sits back of a long, wide valley
ringed with big crags, drained
by a loud, bubbling river.
It is a jewel box of old art:
a carved alabaster triptych,
a Greenland soapstone baptism bowl,
a German wooden Christ in his worst agony.
Here too, under glass, rests
the first printed book in Icelandic—
a heavy Bible, price: one cow.
Under it, the bishop's bones.
Only room here for a few
worshippers at a time—
usually enough space in Iceland.
On this sunny July afternoon,
a soprano sings: Mozart, Bach,
three by Henry Purcell,
accompanied by the awkward organ
that longs to be a harpsichord.
"When I am laid in earth—
remember me," sings Dido.
"Music for a while
shall all your cares beguile—"
"I attempt from Love's sickness to flee."
These old English songs,
so melancholy, so dissonant,
sound oddly right in this room,
with sun streaming over
the forty listening faces, one row
of the old and damaged, tongues
too big for the mouths, faces
asymmetrical, skewed.
But they seem moved as I am,

all our cares beguiled
by the labor of remembering.
The soprano finishes with Bach,
"Aus Leibe will mein Heiland sterben."
"Out of love will my savior die."
Music of exquisite sadness,
weeping, curling counterpoints.
This singing beguiles us, too,
in the pint-sized cathedral
at the end of the earth
on this sunny Sunday afternoon
keeping company with
the old bishop's bones.

Tunnel

Entering a tunnel the first time
you operate on pure faith
that there's another side.
Maybe the sign was just fooling . . .
Maybe it's a trap. Maybe
that light is only a trick after which
the road falls a thousand feet
straight down into the sea.
Notice even rational humans,
like you, for instance, always breathe
a little easier after the road
continues through the mountain
uneventful, down the cliffside
toward what looks from here
like civilization, and maybe is.

Last Meal

On death row you celebrate your last night
with your last dinner, your choice, your last craving
to make at least your stomach happy before it stops
craving anything at all. Many choose
simple food: a hamburger, mac and cheese, ice cream.
What might it be for you, my friend?
Duckling Rouenaisse? A roast of unborn lamb?
Washed down with Veuve Clicquot '59 and old Armagnac?
And how do you know, my friend, that you are not
eating your last meal at this very table now?
Chew slowly. Make sure you take in all the body and the blood.

Glorified Body

We shall return again, says Paul,
In a glorified body, all
Our diseases healed, our lost limbs
Grown again, our gross bellies trimmed.
Kristján's Parkinson's at last stilled,
New pancreases for Eric and Bill,
Leo rises and walks again,
My mother's death wart leaves her skin,
Alec's heart continues beating,
All tumors and wounds retreating.
Now all we have to do is die
To find if Saint Paul told a lie.

New Religion

This morning no sound but the loud
breathing of the sea. Suppose that under
all that salt water lived the god
that humans have spent ten thousand years
trawling the heavens for.
We caught the wrong metaphor.
Real space is wet and underneath,
the church of shark and whale and cod.
The noise of those vast lungs
exhaling: the plain chanting of monkfish choirs.
Heaven's not up but down, and hell
is to evaporate in air. Salvation,
to drown and breathe
forever with the sea.

New Dreams

Now that I'm almost old, I've begun
dreaming of my parents for the first time.
They're both long dead. I thought my dream shop
gave up on them, saying, "That is that."
But no, they arrive now often in the night,
alive in their prime, my father always
in his bib overalls, looking impatient
to get back into the field, my mother
in a brightly colored dress, her hair fixed.
They speak only Icelandic to each other,
probably arguing or telling secrets.
How would I know? Can't follow a word of it.
They're back in dreams for some good reason,
but I will never figure out what it is.
The language of dreams is always Icelandic,
unless it is Latin, Chinese, Hebrew, Sanskrit.

Invisible Guests

I'm gathering half-damp wash from the line in case this heavy
mist emulsifies to rain. Dídí comes bounding out from her café
across the street, pointing and announcing—*"Sjáðu! Hvalur!"*
"Look! Whales!" Two, one next to the harbor, one halfway
across the fjord. By the time I put down my clothespin to look,
they're gone, dived under, heading for open sea. I stare at the
blank mist for a long time, hoping for a splash, a spout, a breach,
a loud whale call, for any evidence of the now invisible. Like any
search for truth or transcendence, this does not go well. If the
messiah came, I'd lift my head a second too late to see it. So we
live and die, always without evidence, but on the lookout, just
in case.

Chinese New Year Feast

At the Chinese New Year table,
dishes arrive in an empty room,
perfume the air with garlic, ginger, chili,
then the doors are closed to allow
the dead to enjoy their dishes in private:
Grandfather's beloved dry-cooked eels,
Father's fish-flavored aubergines,
Auntie's pork belly in red sauce.
They are quiet at table, quick to finish,
conversation does not distract them,
their quarrels long since settled.
The dead are light eaters, thoughtful of us live ones,
hardly touching a morsel or moving a chopstick.
After a seemly time for food to settle,
the dead invite us to follow, to feast
on their leftovers yet another year,
before we begin to join them one by one
in this silent banquet of history, duty, love,
all the dishes that make us human,
the recipes for poems we live and die by.

Alberta Clipper

At twenty below, this wind
has teeth, not a figure
of speech but a fact.
It hungers, not just for cheeks
or fingers or feet.
This zombie zephyr wants
the engine of life itself.
Seized up, stopped dead
as your car is.
Listen to its jaws
clack together on the porch.
Don't open the door.

Seattle

Not every city is lucky enough for
such a volcano to rise behind it
and a few miles above, close
enough that if it decided
to wake from its long sleep,
it could melt, crisp, bury, flood
even the memory of its suburbs,
cathedrals, banks, public monuments,
all vanished for a thousand years
or ten thousand or for good.
All that ash and lava and debris
would make an impregnable sarcophagus
for a million, or five million,
a better morgue than Dresden or Hiroshima.
Our wars only puny bringers of death.
But this! This has grandeur, but no blame.
We were not strong or ruthless enough
to do this to ourselves, so the volcano,
the voice of god, stomach of the earth
spews up at us, as Revelation says,
in the twinkling of an eye.
Such a mountain should keep a city
shy about its standing on earth's skin.

You see it around every corner,
at the top of every rise, at the end
of the long avenue that bears its name,
off the deck of the rich doctor's house
as drinks before dinner arrive
and the important issues are debated
with wit and earnest intention while
the debaters keep one eye always on it.
To genuflect would be too much:
vulgar, superstitious, groveling,
but maybe a tip of the hat, a discreet
nod to acknowledge the end-master,
there, visible, waiting, waiting.

Gait

As a boy, I remember seeing the old
clumping their slow way along Minneota streets,
shuffling, wobbling, cane taps, hunched backs,
as if each step triggered a shooting pain.
Repulsive, I thought, why can't they move
not like an insect, but like something still alive.
I scurried around them, peeved at their dawdling.
But I forgot them, continued my adventures.
Now they are all dead. A half century after,
I've been practicing my personal shuffle,
tempo shrunk from allegro to largo,
tapping the cane to find dry places on the ice,
O Gunnar, Steingrimur, Avy, Abo,
forgive the ignorant and idiotic boy
who did not notice the intricate steps
of the last dance until he practiced himself.

Mozart with Kathleen

At the Christening of Viktor Smári

Mister Viktor Smári arrives on earth
and a few weeks later hears his name
spoken for the first time by his mother in
the presence of assembled relatives.
This is Iceland, where nothing begins to exist
until it has aquired a name:
house, farm, sheep, canyon, glacier, even lava:
Crazy Lava, Foul Deeds Lava, Gray Pants Lava.

So now you've got one, Mister Viktor Smári.
Your new name buzzes up and down the table
as old ladies try it on for size in their mouths.
But what does *Viktor* mean? asks one gray head.
What it says: the big winner, the triumphant,
whether in Eurovision, the World Cup, or life.
It's a lovely word everywhere except in war
where it's never been of any use at all.

For Anna Sigga and Ívar

What song shall we sing to celebrate
the singer's joy who's married and buried
half the city with her bronze voice
and lifted to laughter the spirits of the rest?
Do the bringers of song deserve
a song themselves? Who then will sing
for Ívar and Anna Sigga who have found
love, humor, kindness in each other?
They have, therefore, decided to share
all of it with the rest of us who love them,
generously as they give everything else:
whether Brahms, blues, a fat back of lamb,
or a kiss and a wink for the whole cosmos.
You call this a marriage; I call it a coronation for two.

Happy Fiftieth to Meredith Knox

A woman comes alone from Canada
to this lonesome little town
on the edge of the Arctic.
Her grandmother spoke Icelandic:
now she will try to speak it, too,
but finds it is an easier language
for dead grandmothers than
for live women in the middle of life.
But she's a stubborn one. She persists
through one long, dark winter,
then another, now another yet.
To last those winters requires
desire, and a center inside that
will not wobble in the north wind.
Sanity and grace are her companions
in the rooms she visits. Now
she is rounding fifty, here so far
from where she started. But fifty
is only a small rounding of the bend.
What comes next takes courage, brings
trouble, but, with persistence, ends
with a weird joy—having a whole life.

—Bill Holm (who rounded the bend long ago!)
August 12, 2008

Ragga's Dog

What's a whippet doing in Iceland
with his thin coat, his flying feet?
No fat under that skin to warm him
in a north wind. Nothing to race
with wild abandon here. Slow sheep,
slower cows, placid horses. But keep
running far enough and you'll find the sea
where all the rules for whippets change.
Go to your mistress. Practice your charm
so she'll take you out for a morning scamper
to feel the pulse of speed in your anxious thighs.

Hafrún on Horseback

Hafrún, named for the sea, sits majestically
on her black horse, under her black rider's helmet.
Though she is only nine, barely over
four feet tall, when offered a lift
to the stirrup, she harrumphs with disdain,
throwing her foot up almost past her head
to mount her sleek, half-wild steed.
She sits, straight backed as a small queen
surveying her subjects. She shows off
the trot, the *töllt,* the gallop, the pace.
She has won a horse show this very day,
but says she only hoped to place.
She puts a serious expression on her face.
She will be quite a piece of work at seventeen,
and pure grandeur on horseback at seventy
when we are all long dead, so we must imagine
her now on this summer afternoon by the sea.

Solstice Poem—for Kristján Árnason

Three times in the night
I threw off the quilt
And rushed to the window to stare
At the light on the mountain Tindastoll.
At twelve it was pink
And the snow on the cliffs
Was on fire as if from within.
At four it was gold
And seemed almost to rise from the water.
Every line on its face
Looked like print on a page
Or notes on a musical clef—
And the birds that flew by
Were reading the message
Before diving to tremble the water.
At seven the mountain
Was once again brown,
With wisps of cloud overhead.
Who can sleep on the solstice
When out of the window
This glory of light is erupting?
No wonder the choirs
Of fishers and farmers
All sing with such fire of feeling
Whenever the song
Of the light on the mountain
Rings out from them over the water.
Half a year onward
The light will be scarcer,
The mountain shrouded in snow,
And the birds on the water
Will have gone away, leaving
Only the ghosts of their singing.
But the songs of the choir
To the rhymes of the lovers
Of the light over Tindastoll

Are the storehouse of beauty
When humans most need it
To remind them that everything lovely
Will come back again and again and again
If you keep it in language and music
Alive at the core of your soul.

7:00 AM, June 21, 2007

First Fishing

We watch the video of blonde Sigrún
three years old in pink boots
fishing in the fjord with her *Afi*.
She flashes a gap-toothed grin
while reeling in a wriggling codfish
with a little help from beaming *Afi*.
The fish is half her size.
Soon she will eat part of it
in order to grow old and wrinkled
and, with luck, half-remember
the pleasure of catching something
wet and slick and still alive
surrounded by those who adore you
just for being alive yourself.

Mozart with Kathleen

In honor of your death, my friend Kathleen,
I go to the piano, play half the four-hand Mozart
we worked at for so many years.
The bass is sadder now, because the tune
slid over and off the top of the keyboard
and disappeared in the winter air,
leaving this row of forty ivory slabs
interrupted by black wedges of wood
silent and still as a sculpture garden
closed now for the season. But listen—
the ghost tune still sounds deep
in the caverns of the ear, the ghost hands
still searching for the right fingering.
We'll get it right yet, Kathleen,
but only you and I will ever know or hear.

Storm Coming to Seattle

Hofsós Aubade

The sun bullies its way over the east mountain—
black stones of the harbor, the big blue trawler,
the two white boats, the yellow forklift,
lit suddenly as if by klieg lights
flipped on for the interrogation:
How much cod you take yesterday?
What you up to all night under the fog?
Anything else you need to confess?
Meanwhile the sea turns gold, begins murmuring to itself
as if embarrassed by this loud light.

Fog Cutter

Now the long fog scrims
mountains, clouds, sea,
anything farther away
than a hundred yards.
Through this flies
the oystercatcher
rending the white soup
with his loud red sword
while praising himself
at the top of his lungs.

A Last Word with the Fog

After ten years of whining I'm finally
making friends with the fog.
How courteous of the world out the window
to disappear for a little while.
You, too, can disappear, even in
broad—though murky—daylight.
Only in children's fantasy stories
does the invisibility cloak exist,
and, of course, in Skagafjörður. . . .
Use your disappearance prudently,
as the mountain and the fjord
intend to use their own.
Maybe, with luck, no one will ever
find you again except
yourself, when the fog gives up,
as it always does, and goes away
to give some other lucky fjord
a day or two to disappear.

Sudden Wind Comes to Skagafjörð

At eleven, the southwest wind arrives
with such sudden violence that I imagine
the entire fjord barging straight
through the window to get me.
Such noise! Banging and crashing! All this
after a long, calm day of pale summer light.
Wave tongues licking ever closer—
surf rollers standing upright on their hind legs.
I give up reading my dull book
to admire this ghostly half hurricane.
Maybe, as Revelation says, this is IT!
The Rapture, the Reckoning, Armageddon.
What fun! After all the ballyhoo
it was worth waiting for, but by midnight
it's over, only raining a little.
The four horsemen
will have to make another pass.

Executioner

The north wind today is trying
to break the neck of the grass.
For scaffold music it provides
the whanging tambourine
of the flagpole halyard.

Rhubarb

In this treeless, chilly place,
rhubarb comes early and fast,
shoots out of the ground like a fist,
keeps growing into a forest.
No place else could you use this
excuse for your sudden absence:
"I was lost in the rhubarb forest."

Horses

Go stand by the fence.
Keep quiet. The horses will come—
thirty, forty of them,
however many live and dine there.
They will put their long, narrow noses
one or two at a time
over the fence to nuzzle you,
maybe nibble on your shirt
or suck your finger.
They are watching you
with full attention.
You look curious to them:
docile and harmless.
They want to touch you, pet you,
see what skin feels like.
Don't disappoint them.

Stercorarius Parasiticus

(Kjói—Parasite Jæger—Arctic Skua)

They don't seem birds but acrobats of air,
The dark wings twice too wide to carry their
Ordinary bodies, so they show off
Their stuff like hotdog pilots at the fair,
Dazzling the crowd with wild loop-de-loops,
Or Army pilots sent to save the troops
With dives of derring-do and devil-may-care.
If they had heads that carried caps, they'd doff
Them, take their bows, accept their well-earned praise.
No human eye can watch them without wonder.
Neighbor birds, instead, see them, give chase, they
Know they cannot lose, to bully plunder
From weaker, lesser wings, grab food away
In midair. Power's less pleasing to the prey.

Ice Concert

On solstice night atop the Long Glacier,
almost a mile in the air, the Cathedral Choir,
dressed in puffy orange overalls, toasts
the mountains underfoot with cold schnapps,
then sings a sad lullaby for an outlaw's
drowned daughter and an even sadder
patriotic tune in praise of Mother Iceland,
spread out fifty miles on all sides below.
The children hurl summer snowballs
at their singing parents' orange asses,
but nobody loses either pitch or tune.
They look so silly that I weep.
For these songs the gods
made up the universe.

At Reykir, a "Hot" Farm on the Solstice, 2008

Steam clouds rise out of the bog ditches,
out of the river, out of the grass,
the earth itself warm underfoot.
Fifty horses gallop in the pasture,
warming their bellies and hooves as if
on parade inside a heated hippodrome.
At the farmstead: a homemade church
and a homemade museum in the form
of an old turf house with grass roof.
Inside the farmer's house, the fresh smell
of boiled potatoes and home-smoked mutton.
Two little blonde girls, swathed in pink,
amble outside bareback on placid ponies,
then climb on the grass roof to tumble
back down to the warm mattress of earth,
laughing as if this were a normal way for a child
to pass the long, bright light of the solstice.

Storm Coming to Seattle

White noise of the wind—
rat-a-tatting of rain.
After dark, snow climbs down
lower and lower from the peaks
to the passes, the foothills, the suburbs—
5,000, 2,000, 1,000, 100,
finally over the sea,
where it disappears into itself.

II. Boxelder Bug Variations

It is sometimes difficult to keep in mind that boxelder bugs are not the only amazing and unlikely creatures in the universe

I

"I don't know how anything so dry
as those bugs can be alive."

II

Yahweh, Mohammed, and Jesus
all bloomed in the desert.

III

And the saguaro cactus—
the worst lizards—

Asked why, of all things, I write poems about boxelder bugs, I invoke the ghost of my mother, who had more than her share of Icelandic wisdom

Jona used nylon stockings as rope,
made cats out of beer bottles and light bulbs,
Christmas angels from rolled-up newspapers,
patched the patches on patches on underwear
til they turned into clown suits,
polished shoes with old socks,
and rosemaled coffee cans.
You never know, she said,
when it might come in handy,
and you can always put it in soup
where it'll taste good.
In the '30s, she canned pigeons,
made gravy with chicken feet.
Old, torn pants turned into quilts,
and pillows were stuffed with hair.
Don't waste what little you've got, she said.
Hard times are coming again; someday
you'll be hungry and poor,
sorry for what you throw away
or ignore.

Isak Dinesen, when she was old, dined only on oysters, white grapes, and champagne. The boxelder bug, too, practices a parsimonious though elegant diet

The bug slides
out from behind
the radio dial
where all winter
he lived
eating music.

To continue Emerson's essays *Nature* and *The Poet*

Nature is thrifty; wastes nothing.
There is always the right number
of boxelder bugs, in the right
places. The poet's eye should be
likewise economical. Let him
cease complaining that the world
is without objects fit to become
his subject. He could live two
centuries and not exhaust a
boxelder bug, seen right. The
question is always and only how
quickly a single boxelder bug
would exhaust himself on the
whole tribe of poets.

A lady from Montevideo describes her struggle with boxelder bugs

It started with cold war;
Now we've moved to detente—

The poet recommends surrender.
Then joy.

Minnesota winters are difficult for creatures whose weight cannot be measured in stones

A boxelder bug surprised out
in west wind at forty below
rode swirling snow
clean out of Minnesota,
wound up embalmed in
an ice cube in Pennsylvania,
scared hell out of the lady
who found red stripes in her gin
and tonic, thought she'd seen
the face of God.

Kafka only imagined it

Sometimes I roll over in bed,
think I've turned into one.
They outnumber me by so many,
live more peacefully in my house
than I do myself.
No ghosts for them;
chairs rocking in the dark.
At night, they crawl into me—
carry food and ideas
from brain to thigh
to spleen to finger.
Early in the morning
my hands go by themselves
to the piano, begin
playing music I've never heard before.

Some countries, by virtue of harsh geography and the absence of trees, are deprived of their company

In Iceland
No boxelder bugs

Hungry birds
Lonesome houses

No frogs
Either

Silent water
All night

As a boxelder bug bores inside a maple seed, so do variations burrow into the true music buried at the heart of even so trivial a theme as Anton Diabelli's *Waltz*

Friends, hearing some of these poems, remarked that the connection between boxelder bugs and Beethoven's *Diabelli Variations* is not immediately apparent. This might be true, but only if one had not spent considerable time swatting boxelder bugs off a score while practicing. Pianists understand that both hands are required continually and vigorously to play the *Diabelli Variations*.

I am interested in the *idea* of Variation. It is a curious fact that often the most ingenious and intense pieces by the greatest composers, which seem to accumulate a lifetime's whole knowledge and feeling into themselves, are long sets of variations that begin with trifles, with nothing, and build enormous, sublime, ecstatic, often humorous structures. This is something like building Notre Dame with tinker toys. The architect stands back and smiles, inviting you to admire his fantastic powers. Bach begins with a little dance tune from a child's instruction book and, using the bass line, builds the *Goldberg Variations,* an hour of canons, fugues, dances, laments, bravura displays, and finally, a joke: he combines tune and bass with two vulgar folk tunes: "I Been So Long Without You, Honey," and "Cabbages and Rutabagas Have Driven Me Away." Schumann thinks of a couple of his girl friends' names and home towns, picks out the musical notes that happen to be in them, and makes *Carnaval*. But Beethoven's *Diabelli Variations* are in some ways the grandest and most wonderful of them all.

Diabelli was a commercial promoter in nineteenth-century music publishing, and a kind of composer to boot. He sent out his innocuous little waltz, and invited most of the well-known composers in Europe to contribute variations—proceeds to go to a charity. This is an idea that generally produces second-rate everybody! Beethoven, at his imaginative height in 1820, looked at the little ta-tum waltz with irony and disdain, reading it with deaf ears, but with one of the most powerful musical minds yet born on this planet. On second look, almost to dare himself, he thought: how would this trifle sound if I ground it up in my imagination?

The result, an hour and a half long, is not easy to describe. You study it, read it, play it, listen to it for many years, and it does not stop opening itself to you. This is the bottomless delight of the human intelligence working as well as it probably ever has worked. But it is funny—full of parody, satire, and wit of the broadest and roughest kind! All this sublime humor grows from a simple boxelder bug of a waltz heard from Beethoven's angle.

This is not the *Diabelli Variations*. It is praise of the intelligence and spiritual life that roll around under Beethoven, and, equally, under the boxelder bug; an experiment to see whether something as simple and unpretentious as this bug has the sublime and eternal underneath its wings, holding it up in its long march through this world.

Playing the *Diabelli Variations,* I discover that the sublime is sometimes apparent in the unpretentious, if you listen with the right ears

I

On a piano full of boxelder bugs, I practice the *Diabelli Variations.* Bugs crawl over it, trapped between keys, impaled on hammers, plunging to death under the pedal. Some crawl onto the score, try to make Beethoven into Ives by filling in chords, adding a dissonance or two. I am not fooled. I flick them off lightly, go at C Major like a man possessed.

II

The boxelder bugs waltz, flap their black wings, get their antennae rhythm right, dream of going on the road, giving lessons, getting rich. They understand the C-Major mind, know there are lots of them out there, the boxelder-bug majority, waltzing together forever, reaching for wallets, wings ruffling in unison.

III

This boxelder waltz crawled through cathedral jaws into the whale's stomach, found juices so acid they melted it down into gold. That stomach honors whatever is drowned and transformed inside it. The poor waltz knew it would die, so it ate well before expiring into music.

IV

Beethoven, I love being born on this planet with you: bending over music paper, breath ripe with onions and cabbages, socks moldy on your feet, gray ratty hair falling over your folded forehead, stone ears stuffed with bugs, ear trumpet pointed inside, the barrel exploding with laughter, that peculiar, joyful music of human suffering.

Eleven boxelder bug Haiku

I

Careful if you kill him!
There may be an afterlife
for both of you.

Those black spots in your lamp?
Only bugs who didn't make it
into the next world.

Here's a bug trapped,
dried in a spider web.
Where's the spider?

That bug tickling grandpa's photo
can't tell the difference
between quick and dead. Can you?

Praying to Jesus, I note
the boxelder bug crawl
out of his shadow.

II

"Always tell fall's come—
That shed out back's so full of 'em
she moves around by herself."

"Ma put out coffee cans
full of water. Those bugs thought
they'd found the swimming hole."

III

Don't fret, bug,
I keep house . . .
casually.

Somehow these
boxelder bugs don't seem
Icelandic. . . .
    —Issa (Robert Hass)

IV

The piano string stops trembling
but boxelder bugs
keep dancing.

The boxelder bug—
another thing that will never
be my friend.
    —Basho (Robert Bly)

The history of American poetry, or: Oscar Williams looks at a boxelder bug for *Readers' Digest* books

1

I think I could turn and live with the boxelder bugs.
They are so placid and self-contained.
I stand and look at them long and long.
Boxelder bugs bring me tokens of myself.
I wonder where did they get those tokens?
Did I pass that way huge times ago,
and negligently drop them?

2

So much depends upon a boxelder bug
covered with soap suds beside the white sink.

3

Whose bugs these are I do not know.
His tree is in the village though.
He will not mind me stopping here—
To scoop up bugs before the snow.

4

I was of three minds like a window
In which three boxelder bugs are crawling.
A man and a woman are one.
A man and a woman and a boxelder bug are one.

5

The bug comes in on little bug feet
sits looking over stove and icebox
on silent haunches and then crawls on

6

I, too, dislike them; there are things that are important beyond
    boxelder bugs.
Killing them, however, with a perfect contempt for them, one
    discovers something like affection for the little bastards—
imaginary windows with real boxelder bugs in them.

7

Fat black bugs in a wine barrel room
Barrel house bugs with wings unstable
Sagged and reeled and expired on the table
Boomlay, boomlay, boomlay, BOOM.

8

I thank you God for most this amazing
bug: for the crawling blackly spirits of trees
with a neat, sleek stripe of red, and for everything
which is unwanted, which is numerous, which is no.

9

I'd rather, except for the penalties, kill a man than a bug,
but the small black wing
had nothing left but a feeble wave which said, "Up yours."
I gave him the big thumb in the twilight.

10

What happens to a bug in a window?
Does it dry up like a raisin in the sun
Or does it explode?
No. It eats in the kitchen and grows strong.

How they die

They dry up,
turn into light.

To explain my unusual interest in boxelder bugs, particularly those who live in my piano

I

I love whatever is difficult to kill:
Whales, grizzly bears, snapping turtles, boxelder bugs, some
    human beings,
Old Viking stories about corpses that won't stay dead.

I love stones that rest uneasy in the earth;
Boulders grunted up after the glacier;
Rock so anxious to see daylight, it bubbles out of volcano mouths.
I love water that freezes, takes a long time, and makes noises
Belching, snoring, moaning, sneezing, before spring melt.

I love old houses and barns that weather and lean into themselves.
You hear wind without opening the door.
The dresser leans forward.
Pictures slide to odd angles on the wall.
Weather comes, a guest, inside;
Still they refuse to fall unless
Beaten with crowbars and hammers.

II

You can kill anything by working at it;
The whole world of tame animals, dammed rivers,
Iron barns, tight houses, polished stones, helpful psychologists,
Heated pools, and half-dead people,
Wants you to join it,
Mails you invitations every day,
Each one more cordial and demanding.
Ignore them, and they grow hysterical, and will kill you.
Believe me, they can do it, and furthermore will be rewarded
    for it.
There is a bounty on *you.*

III

I was one hundred years old the day I was born, and knew all
these things without words.
I felt it the first time I heard Beethoven played on a scratchy old
record player.
I felt it the first time I opened my eyes at a funeral and saw that the
corpse and I were the only two people alive in a full church.
I felt it at eleven years old when I bought Walt Whitman's poems
for $3.50 in Sioux Falls.
I fingered the book for a long time, knowing inwardly someone
had come close.
I feel it now, early in the morning the way the *Art of Fugue* moves
around under my fingers on an old piano.

IV

Most of all, I love an old piano that refuses to die,
To be thrown in the chicken coop, chopped apart with an ax;
A patient piano that develops a sense of humor after sixty years,
A few water marks, a few scratches, a clatter in the bushings as felt
Hardens like an artery, a string going dead now and then.
This piano kept itself lean, doesn't eat much,
Its voice darkened and mellowed since 1922.
It plays noisy music quietly, quiet music like feathers dropped
in a well.
It's fit for Bach now, and music by old men.
It likes human beings and is kind to them,
Doesn't even mind boxelder bugs that live in it.
This piano will die, too, but not before saving many times the
odd man who plays it,
Sometimes gets out of bed late at night to feel its keys in the dark.

Though we flatter ourselves as individualists, there is always another part that suspects the contrary truth

I

All alike, they disappear
into each other's lives,
without detection;
one wing black as the other,
each stripe red as the next.
Death doesn't happen
bug by bug,
but by season.

II

With us it's different, we think,
each raised to be odd,
the center of his own world,
without which nothing else is;
and it all goes down
with a burst of weeping,
a hollow space in the air
where our body stood.

III

Sometimes I long
to disappear, be one
of millions wearing
the same wings, crawling
in the same window, sitting
in a room full of others,
invisible, have them wonder what
was his name? No matter. . . .

Driving past Westerheim Graveyard (Jonina Sigurborg Josephson Holm, June 23, 1910–May 25, 1975)

You must be dry as a spring boxelder bug by now
In your underground house;
Nothing but bones and a husk.
The rest stands, like the bug,
Next to the coffee pot,
Ready to tell stories.

You always knew it would happen this way.
Even when you are not in a room, you are
In it, your voice everywhere,
Under cushions, back of the stove,
Coming out from mouths of painted figurines.
Your breath still blows dust around
Under bric-a-brac.
Eyes on the pictures blink.

Each fall, new bugs crawl in,
Make pests of themselves again
In the same old way.
They look just like last-year's batch.
Maybe they are.
I don't have to tell you these things.

III. The Dead Get By with Everything

Icelandic Graveyard, Lincoln County

A woman and I go to the immigrant graveyard
on top of a bare and windy prairie hill.
She's never been here, but she sees
her own name on every headstone:
Svanhilder, Svandís, Svanhvít, the swan
who died sometimes an old lady flocked
by children, grandchildren, great-grandchildren,
petals grown up around a flower.
Sometimes she died a child who couldn't talk,
gone away without God's water on her head.
Sometimes the name spelled right, sometimes not.
It's good to die so many times, she says,
to feel the death shuddering in your bones
so often; when muscles practice this well
they move with a dancer's delicate grace.

At the Writers' Conference

After my rambunctious verbal assault
on two thousand years of Christian baggage,
three thousand of European mistakes,
a sprightly, pin-curled old lady with sad eyes
asks: "Why do you call it Christian baggage?"

This conversation can't go on. We both know it.
How do I explain in three minutes
why everything has been dead wrong
since the beginning?
Authority made of paper, strategy in vestments,
charity wearing sidearms, risen corpses,
virgin mothers, just armies . . . Damn the logic!

My baggage is her furniture; she lives
in my fire sale, serves tea every day in thin
blue porcelain cups that she imagines me
smashing one after the other
with arrogant clumsiness, tossing them into
the fearful darkness outside her parlor window.

Rose Bardal

Rose, her face pinched toward God,
used to disappear during church picnics.
The men spread out in the field until
they found her preaching in Icelandic
to the cornstalks with a loud voice.
They always brought her back before
she converted the corn
which stood unrepentant
waiting for the picker or the hailstorm.

She wrote to the Pope in 1939
demonstrating to him clearly
the error of his opinions, giving him,
in calm prose, one more chance
to be a Lutheran.
Her sister found the letter
before Rose found a stamp
and hid it away,
unsealed but addressed,
until after they both were dead.
I found it, ready to go to:
MR. PIUS XII, VATICAN, ROME, ITALY, EUROPE.

Maybe I'll mail it forty years late,
see if it works, maybe the ones
to Hitler, Roosevelt, Stalin too.
While the rest of the world waited
like zombies for another mound of corpses,
this crazed woman saw God's hand
moving among corn leaves, firmly
pulling out the cockleburs.

A Circle of Pitchforks

(A poem about the farmers' protest against a
proposed power line through Pope County, Minnesota)

I

They used to call it a sheriff's sale.
Had one over by Scandia in the middle of the '30s.
My dad told me how
the sheriff would ride out to the farm
to auction off the farmer's goods for the bank.
Neighbors came with pitchforks
to gather in the yard:
"What am I bid for this cow?"
Three cents. Four cents. No more bids.
If a stranger came in and bid a nickel,
a circle of pitchforks gathered around him
and the bidding stopped.
Even in the gray light of memory
the windmill goes around uneasily,
the farmer's overalls
blow into the fork tines,
the striped overalls look like convict suits.
A smell of cow shit and wet hay seeps into everything.
The stranger wears tweed clothes
and a watch chain.
The sheriff's voice weakens
as he moves from hayrack to hayrack
holding up tools,
describing cattle and pigs
one at a time.
The space between those fork tines
is the air we all breathe.

II

"Resist much, obey little,"
Walt Whitman told us.

To bring the light!
That's the thing!
Somewhere in North Dakota
lignite gouged out of the prairies
is transformed into light.
But you are not in darkness, brothers,
for day to surprise you like a thief.
We are all sons of the light,
sons of the day;
we are not of the night,
or of darkness.
Let us not sleep, as others do
but keep awake and be sober.
Those who sleep,
sleep at night,
and those who get drunk,
are drunk at night.

III

There is so much light in Minnesota:
the white faces brought here from Arctic Europe,
the lines of white birch in the white snow,
white ice like a skin over the water,
even the pale sun seen through snow fog.
White churches, white steeples, white gravestones.

Come into an old café
in Ghent, or Fertile, or Holloway.
The air is steamy with cigarette smoke and frozen breath,
collars up under a sea of hats pulled down.
You can hardly see the mouths moving under them.
The talk is low, not much laughing.
Eat some hot dish, some Jell-O,
and have a little coffee and pie.
These are the men wrecking the ship of state—

the carriers of darkness.
Up in the cities
the freeway lights burn all night.

IV

My grandfather came out of Iceland
where he took orders from the Danes and starved.
After he died, I found his homestead paper
signed by Teddy Roosevelt,
the red wax still clear and bright.
In the corner, a little drawing of a rising sun
and a farmer plowing his way toward it.
A quarter section, free and clear.
On his farm he found arrowheads
every time he turned the soil.
Free and clear. Out of Iceland.
In the '30s, the farm was eaten by a bank
thrown back up when Olson
disobeyed the law that let them gorge.
In high school they teach
that Hubert Humphrey was a liberal
and Floyd Olson is a highway.

V

Out on the power line barricades,
the old farmers are afraid their cows'
teats will dry up after giving strange milk,
and their corn will hum in the granary all night.

They have no science, no words, no law,
no eminent domain
over this prairie full of arrowheads and flowers,
only they know it,
and the state does not.

We homestead in our bodies too,
a few years, and then go back
in a circle
faster than the speed of light.

Under Holdrege, Nebraska

I skip stones into billowing Nebraska wheat
as if it were a rolling golden ocean.
One nips the beard in seven arcs until
it cuts into a breaker and sinks.
No telling how far that stone will drop.

Sin in Utah

for Jan and Dave Lee

In Utah, it is probably illegal
even to think it, much less commit
whatever it was, though in this
great emptiness of canyons, you will
probably get by with it
for a while—if nobody sees;
but if you don't do it, as Joe Hill
almost certainly didn't, they will still
shoot you for it, and music
to the contrary, you will then
be dead, or if you did it partly
and partly didn't, like John D. Lee,
the Mormon massacrer and ferry man,
they will try you once and let you off,
and a quarter century after
it has made any difference,
try you again, and hang you
for it; in Utah even not
thinking about it may not save you,
so you might as well do it. Most do.

Grand Canyon of the Colorado

This big emptiness is the hollow under
your bed at three years old where something
too fast for light waits to chew at you.

It's the hole under the pasture that cows
know about before a tornado. At night,
there's an invisible river a mile underfoot.

Watch the tourists, brave with cameras
at sundown, cowering away from the silence
flooding up at them through the dark.

Here we're all children waiting on a branch
for the sound of something climbing up
from the hole nothing should ever get out of.

The Decline of the Colorado

At Yuma, a retired accountant with prostate trouble
could piss across the Colorado.
"Used to be in the canyon business,"
the river whispers, squishing
along between cottonwoods,
"before I moved to California
to grow organic lettuce."

What does a man say to a river
that couldn't flood a ballpark after
a hundred thunderstorms?
Old geezer, it doesn't help—
my weeping for you.

Losing My Billfold in Oregon

I keep losing my billfold; first in a crayfish bar in Portland. The money is gone, but the cards come back, turned in to a cop on a commuter train. My friends think I should be happy at this odd good luck, but instead, I'm a little melancholy. It's me I'm probably trying to lose . . . I'm nearing fifty now, have been Bill Holm long enough. Without money, I can't buy anything, but suddenly now I want nothing I have to pay for. Without cards, I'm nobody except who I say I am, and that can change— all change in an eye blink.

A few days later, walking down a long beach between the Oregon dunes and the noisy Pacific surf, I feel in my pocket. Gone again! Maybe I threw it to the sea when I wasn't looking. Better the tide should have it . . . Rent a car, buy dinner, have a good time with my stone in its pocket. I didn't even know until now how little I wanted that wallet, that life in America, until the sea helped me understand by being something else, clear and loud.

Summer Sunday in Seyðisfjörður

Long silence in this Icelandic farm kitchen;
the Last Supper carved in skin,
gathered all afternoon around the table
to drink just ten more drops of coffee,
clean up cake crumbs one by one.
Everyone asks no one once or twice
if it's time yet to cut the hay.
This only starts silence again
broken apart by in-sucking breath
and *yow-yow* once in a while.
Nobody knows what to affirm, but they
affirm it anyway as if to affirm
the habit of affirming something.
We all look out the window, wait
for cold Atlantic fog to swallow up
the basalt mountains one more time,
leave a blank sky over the sea.
You can still see two rock arms
opening up at the mouth of the fjord.
I want to shout: Europe is out there!
The Last Supper wants to listen;
but no one says anything as fog
folds the fjord into itself again.

Advice

Someone dancing inside us
has learned only a few steps:
the "Do-Your-Work" in 4/4 time,
and the "What-Do-You-Expect" waltz.
He hasn't noticed yet the woman
standing away from the lamp,
the one with black eyes
who knows the rumba
and strange steps in jumpy
rhythms from the mountains of Bulgaria.
If they dance together,
something unexpected will happen.
If they don't, the next world
will be a lot like this one.

Warm Spell

A long November warm spell;
all the blizzards still asleep.
Bees hum unbelieving
around still-blooming flowers.
Leaves, piled in compost heaps,
move around uneasily.
The dried branch bends down
in warm wind,
inviting them home again.

People who haven't spoken in years
smile and greet each other in the street.
Relatives forget old quarrels
over family heirlooms.
The town atheist admits that God exists;
and the town drunk drinks coffee on his porch.
The Lutheran minister forgets
St. Paul, and the furrows
vanish from around his mouth.
Children are conceived in the open air
under willow trees by the river.

Like the life in the body,
this cannot last, so everyone
wastes time joyfully,
not even remembering
the old wounds they gave their spirit.
The old man on the stoop
in front of the beer joint
remembers his first lover,
and his toes begin dancing
around inside his shoes.

Weather

Early November in Minnesota.
Warm, bright days, clear nights—
everyone knows what's coming
so their faces glow
like the fading pictures of saints in old churches.
Cattle lie down in long rows
in the feed lot, stare
silently at the sunlight, licking
each other now and then
with long, rough tongues.

I feel that tongue now—
a river of sand moving up and down my back.
I want to make love on a grassy hill,
no one but cows for miles around;
no sound but mooing and wind in grass;
dance under the boxelder tree;
leap and splash in the river:
a hungry old carp catching flies.

The afterlife must be like this—
a gift I stopped waiting for
that suddenly came, so I praise
dark-eyed women; hillsides
full of blood-red rose hips;
nights so clear stars count
each other, glow like golden
nails in a polished ebony board.

Soup

I come back to my house after seeing her,
this lover of ladybugs, stones, and weeds.
In the refrigerator, I find the bones of a duck,
a little meat still clinging here and there.
Into the iron pot I put the duck,
dried peas, onions, carrots, wine,
prairie sage picked in November sun
from meadows next to Lac Qui Parle.
As I shred the sage, geese begin to honk,
flying low over treetops, gold light
glowing through their wings. Soon
the iron pot boils, and the house
fills with the smell of soup.
I remember the feeling of this woman,
her hands, this pot of soup,
the rush of white tails through the bare woods,
black vines hanging from the boxelders—
the heart swinging back and forth in the body.

Black Duck Love Song

for John and Lorna Rezmerski

The sign in front
of the fiberglass duck
in the Black Duck Park
reads: "Keep off the Duck."
I don't. Part of the world
is like that. Someone
makes something odd.
Someone else puts up
a sign that says:
"Don't finger the bread.
Don't squeeze the tissue.
Keep off the grass.
Break it and you bought it."

Some people don't pay
any attention to signs;
touch each other anyway,
bend, chip, maybe break,
ride black duck wings
onto the statue's eyebrow,
hang glide illegally down
into the canyon they
never noticed before,
handling each other in
the most remarkable way.

Old Sow on the Road
for Walt Gislason

Thirty below. A hundred miles from home
the Buick throws a rod. Dead.
An hour later, I'm headed south
away from Paynesville in a truck.
A half mile out an old sow sits
on broken haunches in the middle
of the road. We stop. Maybe
fell off a stock truck: nobody
saw her in the iced-up mirror.
She swivels on that broken back, a pink
lazy Susan turning on the yellow line.
Ice blue light, gun barrel pavement,
pink nose, snow, snow, more snow.
Airy colors for such a monster painting.
Windows iced tight, heater purrs loud,
but by God, I hear the howling
of that old sow, snout rotating, a double-
barreled gun aimed straight at me.
And that face! That face said everything
I'll ever say until I'm either dead
or alive as that sow at that moment
wanted so badly to be.

Turtle

I

After the turtle was long dead,
body roasted and eaten, head
buried in a shallow grave, a dog
dug it up, found jaws
opening, closing, powerful enough
to bloody his nose.

II

Hindus imagine the world held
delicately on trunk tips
of four elephants standing on
an ancient turtle's back.

Turtle is the oldest life,
has no intention of evolving
toward anything; therefore
is mother of everything.

Turtle celebrates love with
a long, joyful roaring that is
a god's voice inside him.

Scientists don't know
how long he lives, quite
how he dies. Good.

III

Look into a snapping turtle's eye
who suspects you are about to eat him.

A turtle in Wilno, Minnesota,
dined on chickens in a farmer's yard,

reaming them apart with pincer gums.
The blood and feather trail
lead to the pond.

"Wally," the farmer said,
"you eat turtle;
come get him."

IV

At Wally's Wilno tavern
Adeline says, "Got a big snapper
out back, over thirty pounds."

"Can I see him?" I ask.

We walk behind the barroom.
With a five-gallon pail
she dips water from a barrel:
"You can see him better now."
Wally sticks a two by four
into the barrel. A neck shoots
from the gnarled shell;
jaws grab at air.

I would lie if I said
we understood one another,
but he wanted my hand,
and I think I loved him;
white claws, finger size,
gouged on the board;
leather muscles taut
at joints, tongue shot
out in silent howling.

V

"He'll be a bastard to kill," she says.
"I'll hold out a piece of meat,
and when he goes for it,
Wally'll get the head in a pincers
and I'll saw it off at the neck.
But he won't die yet!
Damn things live without the head!
We nail him to a tree and bleed him
twelve, fourteen, sixteen hours;
kill him at night—by God!
Next morning those claws will
still be grabbing out at you.

"So I pull the claws out, skin him;
he'll dress out about twenty pounds;
soak him a day or two in salt water;
brown him in a little butter and flour
and roast him in a big pan."

VI

Uninterested in words
turtle says nothing.

VII

An old Indian had a snapper
who searched out drowned bodies like
a truffle pig snuffling under an oak.
He'd row to the middle of the lake,
drop the snapper with wire
coiled to its thorny tail;
when the wire snapped taut
they rowed straight to the body.

VIII

Turtle saw dinosaur thump
on earth, pulled
inside his ribs, waiting
for something to change.

After a hundred million years,
when thunder lizards lie
pickled in fossil beds,
turtle still opens his box,
puts out his head
into the smoky air.
If he sang, he'd sing:

> "Size did not suffice;
> fur got you nowhere.
> Patience of soul,
> not power, survives.
> My box filled
> with light—"

IX

This is not a riddle.
Turtle is turtle;
will clip off your finger
if you doubt it.
But he is the dead, too,
who will not let go,
poke out their heads
from under our hard
body at all
the strangest hours.

The Dead Get By with Everything
for Alec Bond, 1938–1985

I

I talk to the dead in the middle of the night,
raising my voice when they don't answer.
Maybe they speak a foreign language now.
I feel like an old Spaniard shouting at a Mayan,
asking over and over on what strange shore I'd landed,
while he stands mute and ironic
in the presence of a crescendo of gibberish.
No wonder the old explorers killed everything
that wouldn't speak to them in their own tongue.

II

Dead on Wednesday,
classes as usual Thursday,
clean the office Friday;
a new job to advertise
since you gave up tenure
for this unexcused leave of absence.
I suppose tenured jobs are hard
to come by in the next world too.
You should have made arrangements just in case
you may decide there's nothing smarter
there than here, and come back
to clean your office up at last.
I'd like to see what the contract
says about that, and the expression
on whatever face rummages
at your desk when you amble in
to finish the job before departing
under boot soles and up toward sun,
disembodied, triumphant, dead.

III

It's a bad winter; snow after snow,
ice storms and gale winds between.
Far below zero, door handles crack,
car defroster clogged with ice,
still not Thanksgiving yet,
six months to mosquito hatch.
But you who hated it so much,
a Tennessee man like Sam McGee,
escaped by dying just before it all began.
You missed all these threats on your life
by not having one left to threaten.
It's your fault I feel this shivering
in the valves of my own heart.

IV

In a long dying, you eat what you love
a little at a time, a few bites a day,
and when the plate goes away from the table,
empty, there's a feeling of satisfied desire.
You have finished whoever is gone
and can hear that name spoken
without weeping. You come when called,
do their business, and after a while
it all seems so easy that you add their names
to your own. You take their tax deductions,
answer their mail. When it's time to clean the closets,
you wonder why you bought clothes
that hang so strangely on your body.
You sigh and send on boxes to the starving,
who can wear out whatever life is left
in the overcoat. Meanwhile, you wear out the soul
that never got properly used up.

But with a sudden dying, it's different.
You go to bed with a full, innocent stomach,
and wake to discover your skin's
too small for the whale you swallowed in your sleep.
You try to throw it up, but it won't come.
That dying is inside you for good.
It will be slow digesting—months, even years,
before that protein makes its way
toward where it always goes—
to the grass and the irises, the pigeons
and the snow. You moan from bloat, complain
to the sofa that you sink too far into its cushions.
Your own dog snarls at you.
Nothing can be done about this.

V

Who do the dead think they are!
Up and dying in the middle of the night,
leaving themselves all over the house,
all over my books, all over my face?
How dare they sit in the front seat of my car,
invisible, not wearing their seat belts,
not holding up their end of the conversation,
as I drive down the highway
shaking my fist at the air all the way
to the office where they're not in.
The dead get by with everything.

Brahms' Capriccio in C Major, Opus 76, No. 8

for Marcy

All this lonesome fall I practice Brahms, mooning over a faraway woman, while my fingers twist around this constipated soulful counterpoint. Day after day of gray drizzle, both in October and inside the piano. I don't even like this music and haven't touched a note of it for years.

Tonight, I remember when I played it last; it was the melanoma ward of a huge gray hospital, a whole hallway chock full of the doomed. An old upright piano sat in the sun room, where I waited day after gray drizzly spring day for news I had already gotten inside. I had only Brahms along, and he seemed all right, so I practiced playing and grieving together, conscious of the one, avoiding the other.

Up and down the hall walked glucose bottles attached to bodies. All over those bodies, black holes in the skin sucked up life and energy, burrowing inside from eye, back, hand, cheek, slow black bullets whose trajectory stopped only when they found a brain or liver to explode.

"A nasty disease," the Chinese neurosurgeon said. "We don't know what causes it. Perhaps the sun . . . Probably the sun . . ."

Maybe gray drizzly north German counterpoint so dense the sun can't make its way inside could slow it down a little.

Without much hope for either music or survival down this hall, I practice Capriccios and Intermezzos that old Brahms probably composed while his own black holes ate at his liver. One day, I sit bungling through something in C Major when a young boy with freckles, red hair, and a glucose bottle slides noiselessly into the sun room and listens. He claps weakly when I finish, and I turn around. The glucose bottle still wobbles on its iron stand, the plastic tube trembling.

He is my color, could be my brother, but he is thin, pale, dying, and I am fat, flushed, full of angry life. "I always wanted to play the piano," he said.

"Do it!" I said. "It's a great joy to play."

"Did it take you long to play so well?" he asked.

"Oh, not long at all!" I said. "Just practice all you can."

Then with a weak excuse, I left the sun room, went and sat next to my mother's bed and wept, because I had lied, and because I knew what happened in this world as inexorably as Brahms' ruthless logical contrapuntal knots tied and untied themselves around the human ear.

For twelve years, I forgot those Capriccios and Intermezzos, and neither lied not wept too much. But all this lonesome fall, I practice Brahms again, mooning over a faraway woman I love— no, over two women, one gone out, and the other just come in, the old grief and this new joy so alike inside this music. One brave melody in C, clear and full of leaping rhythm, rears up against a minor tune as if to say: Let everything sing together inside you, lose nothing.

IV. Playing the Black Piano

Bach in Brimnes

Stebbi brings his cello into Brimnes.
He is a big thick fellow with ham fists,
Who looks like a seaman or a deck hand
More used to tubs of fish than cello bows.
No scores here, so he plays what he knows:
Bach! Let's have some Bach! Play a saraband!
The cello seems too big for this small room
But when he starts the Saraband in G,
The whole house grows too tiny for the tune,
As if the walls demanded to expand
Another fifty meters toward the sea
To make a proper space for all this sound,
If any human space at all could house
The planets whirling round inside this suite.

Summer Light in Brimnes

A few miles from this window on the fjord
sits Drangey, the sheer-cliffed island where
Grettir the unlucky hero hid from law
but mostly from the dark.

When night came back to end the summer light,
Grettir swam four miles through freezing water
to find fresh fire after his lumpish servant
let the only embers flicker out and die.

The story's been told for seven hundred years
of this fierce man who fought trolls, ghosts, bears,
but was afraid to sleep without a fire
to burn away the specters in the dark.

Goethe, on his deathbed, said: "More light,"
and painted every room he wrote in white.
Almost old, I've come here to stay
the summer in this cottage without shades.

Here, whenever I roll over in my bed
and wake up in the middle of the night,
it is day, whatever any clock may say,
since my first sight is always light.

The solid world there to greet me,
water, grass, the island, sky,
just where I left them to sleep a while,
the illusion of eternity—

if not the fact. Like Grettir I depend
on darkness to arrive,
on whatever light I gather in to end;
however long a swim I make for fire.

Icelandic Recycling on a Summer Night
for Wincie

Toward midnight, the sky pinks up.
The low cloud at the bottom of Tindastoll
turns the color of wild grapes.
Inside four women sit around a table,
oblivious to natural phenomena,
folding plastic bags
into neat white triangles.
"Ever so much nicer to store!"
They are performing women's work:
Tidying up the garbage
until it looks like modern sculpture.
They have seen it all before:
midnight sun, revolution, disease, chaos.
Their female wisdom comprehends
there is nothing to be done about chaos,
except bring order and harmony
to plastic bags as if they were
wandering children needing to be tucked
in neatly for the long night.

To Kristján Árnason

"I am a poet in words and wood,"
says Kristján Árnason at more than seventy
as he presents me with a wooden bowl
he has made at his house at Skálá,
a farm almost on the Arctic Circle.
In two thousand and one,
if you say in poem or song to your fellow man:
"This is a beautiful bowl," they laugh,
saying: "That is only your view, your denial
that trees have suffered, that one bowl
is necessarily more beautiful than
another bowl." They want an ironic
bowl, not a wooden bowl full of poetry,
but Kristján, a carpenter by trade,
never studied such fashionable stuff,
instead makes beauty from whatever
he finds at hand. He makes his poems
from whichever language he pleases,
bowls of words in English, Danish,
his own beloved Icelandic, which has been
filling bowls with beauty for a thousand years.
Here is a bowl of weather, a bowl of longing,
a bowl of mountains, a bowl of light,
a bowl of thought, a bowl of laughter.
A man does not study to make bowls,
or get a license or certificate.
He makes one after another until
they come right. Words, too, start coming
right if you make them every day for fifty years,
even on farms, so far from the world
of power and fame. Just as your bowl,
if you make it well, holds water
or pens or chocolate or agates,
so will your poems hold beauty
and wisdom and humor and love,

whatever language you make them in,
like the bowls of poems in words and wood
made by Kristján Árnason, *skáld* of Skálá
who made these gifts to me.

Heavenly Length

Schubert does go on, doesn't he?
Don't you find him a bit much?
How much wine is enough
to wash down the bread?
Is there water enough to cover
the barges under Lake Superior?
Does the sun put out too much light?
Are there enough words
in the dictionary yet?
Too many teeth in the whale's jaw?
How many beautiful women
is too many? Will the men find them?
How much Schubert is too much?
Is it far from your left ear
to the top of the Greenland ice?
How many breaths do you intend
to breathe before you die?
Do you want these questions answered?
Someone is singing a long song.
Careful! It's getting inside.

The Man Who Threw Nothing Away
for Leonard Vader

My old friend Leonard believed in throwing nothing away, either inside or outside except maybe Republicans and the lust for money, so he stayed alive an entire eighty years. In America, some die at forty, most by fifty or sixty, though they go on driving cars and expressing opinions for decades while their visible graves, already lined with concrete, await them and their goods. Leonard believed in healthy chickens, proper gardens, rich compost, scrap lumber, the intelligence of children, and that much in this universe can be fixed with duct tape but little with money. He filled his garage with broken parts and single gloves, because you never know when things might come in handy.

From one angle a small man, from another, he grew huge as he aged by sporting a fine white mustache, never forgetting a story, and falling in love every day till he was past eighty. The interior man grew heavier, wiser, even happier, till the earth itself started singing loud songs to beckon him down inside it. The earth wanted better company than humans had been giving it lately.

On a fine damp Bellingham morning, Leonard went with a spade to open his compost heap, his joy and visible emblem of the man who saves everything. When he dug in, a cloud of fine steam billowed up around his snowy mustache while the tabernacle chorus of the compost sang to him in twelve harmonic parts of loud silence: Come, from this we rise, to this we go, from this we come again. Inside our rotting, vibrant heart, your whole life churns and steams, waiting for you to join it. You have ripened like fine late grapes, full of unexpected sugar and flavor. Now it's time to become wine for a while. You saved everything to grow wise. Now it's time for us to save you for a century or two.

Two women who loved him took pictures of that steam and the look on his face that might even be transfiguration, but maybe only wryness, for he knew and they knew what others didn't, that once more, nothing is being thrown away at all.

Playing Haydn for the Angel of Death

for Ethel Pehrson and Tomas Tranströmer

1

The piano tells things to your hands
you never let yourself hear from others:
Calm down, do your work, laugh,
love reason more, your mask less.
God exists, though not as church said.
To understand this language, you must
sometimes patiently play the same
piece over and over for years, then
when you expect nothing, the music
lets go its wisdom.

2

Play Haydn. First, when I was young,
he seemed simple, even simpleminded;
too easy, too thin, too cheerful,
gaiety and dancing in a powdered wig;
no hammer blows at unjust fate,
no typhoons of passion dropping tears,
only laughter, order, invention,
the simple pleasure of ingenuity,
of making something from next to nothing.

3

All the geniuses have their own feel
inside the fingers. Mozart steps to center
stage, takes a long breath, then
sings his aria, but Haydn is skinny
under the hands; all the fat lives
in the spaces between the lines.

You sense that fat jiggling like
Buddha's belly but can't touch it.
After a while, you can hear it when
the notes pass lightly by each other.

4

But O, the mystery of Haydn is
the great reason for not dying young,
for living through rage and ambition
without quite forgetting their pleasures.
Suicide, craziness, the bottle, war—
all rob you of what is inside Haydn.
Take this advice: toughen up and live.
Fifty is a good year; by this time
something has probably happened, and with luck
it has tuned and readied the strings inside you.

5

At fifty, my own life has not come
to much and my death sits in
a straight-back chair under a lilac bush
in the garden behind my house,
reading my old letters, waiting.
He is in no hurry to come knock
on the back door. There's plenty to keep him
interested in the piles of my past
foolishness. Yours, too. On the other hand,
he has no intention of going
elsewhere, just wants to make sure
I notice him, every day, alert
in his straight-back chair.

6

Open the windows. Go to the piano.
Play a Haydn sonata for him. Begin
with an easy, simpleminded one:
Allegretto Innocente, just a tune
and a few variations, all in G,
the key of lessons for little fingers.
Haydn stays in it endlessly to see
what can be said with almost nothing.

7

Thirty years ago, I thought this
a trifle; now here I am playing it
for Death sitting in a straight-back chair.
You think he wanted Wagner maybe?
Or Schoenberg? Some dark, thick Brahms?
What kind of idiot do you think Death?
If he can't hear what's inside Haydn,
how will he manage to throttle your heart?
That takes power, craftiness, patience.

8

Years ago, I wrote about Bach:
"Whoever loves G major loves God."
Truer than I knew, but I didn't say
quite enough: G major is one
of God's eyes through which he watches
hair go gray, or an ear that hears
the cracks in your own singing.
Remember, God and you have two of each
that watch and listen in two directions.

9

Has the angel heard enough G now?
G sings to life only half the earth
or half the truth. Go as far
away from G major as can be gone;
C# minor, the shadow, the nether tone,
but neither Ludwig's moonlight horsefeathers
nor Rachmaninov's gloomy thumping.
Too many wet sleeves and drooping heads.

10

Play Haydn where two gods have a civil talk
while they put the world together.
Haydn gives you two of everything:
two hands, two staves, two keys, two tunes,
two answers to all your questions.
What sits in the garden knows this.

11

For God *is* the imagination.
God made you up entirely, and you
have returned him the favor.
God imagined G major, C# minor.
Now, like Haydn, go and do likewise.
Make a surprise that stays a surprise
to please the ears and spirit of the one
who sits alert in the straight-back chair
under the lilac bush in the garden.

12

Having put the halves of the universe
back in order, it's time to dance—
a minuet, old-fashioned, but a dance
is a dance after all. You used to do
the minuet yourself, didn't you,
a few hundred years ago?
Remember the steps? Here's a good one:
Minuetto Giacoso in C.
You'll like the tune. Careful on the upbeat.
Put a lilac in your buttonhole.

13

When Haydn's own angel of death came
calling in Vienna, he found the old man
with worn-out wits, almost ready
to answer the door. But Death listened:
"I count my life backward now,
and for a few moments I'm young again.
I ought to play for you. Do you want to hear
something of mine?" Then Haydn played, slowly,
Gott! Erhalte Franz den Kaiser.
His wet, rheumy eyes glistened.
"I must play this song every day.
I feel well while I'm playing it,
and for a while afterward, too."

14

The world, though shriveled, remained in order,
so Death stayed away for years,
sat on his street-corner stool and listened.
Even Haydn could do no better
than playing Haydn to keep his guest amused.

15

As music drifts out the open windows,
Death is dancing around his straight-back chair
under the lilac bush in the garden,
trying to make the left foot move in time.
Soon he will be tired out but happy;
he will nap a while and stay away.

That's the idea. I got it from Haydn.

The Weavers

for Don and Mim Olsen

They play a piano made entirely of string,
a tune of whirrs, and clunks, and ratchets,
the music gradually turning blue, gray, pink,
marked by diamonds, flowers, and stars.

One passes a wooden shoe under the strings,
then clunks on her damper pedal.
The shoe goes back and forth, under and through.
It's the shoe of the invisible dancer
who pirouettes on one bare foot
somewhere inside the loom.
The choreography of her toes
weaves diamonds into the blue cloth.

In a thousand years
tapestry will turn into music,
marble into language,
colors into movement, and men
will all be reborn as women and give birth
to themselves over and over again
at a loom, weaving a shirt
to cover the breasts of someone they love.

Glenn Gould, 1932–1982

A man who played the piano with as much genius as it is possible to contain in a human being said he trusted machines and electricity more than he trusted humans in a room. Henceforth, he would play only for steel wire and thin tape, genius saved from coughing, wheezing, and all possibility of disagreeable whispers and remarks.

He took his first machine, the piano, and chiseled, filed, and muffled it until it suited his music and was like no other such machine on earth—a name brand of one. He sat on his second machine, an old chair that squeaked and rocked and comforted him.

He waited until the middle of the night to have perfect silence for his music, then moved his two peculiar machines into a sealed, sound-locked room where not even the vibration of a human foot could ever be felt. There he played, safe at last from the rest of us, and even, he thought, from himself.

But when Bach or Haydn came on him, he started singing in a low and ugly hum, out of tune with everything his hands were doing. No machine could take this noise away or clear it out without losing the music, too, so he was left with an awful choice. Give up principle or give up beauty.

He chose the music, hums and all, a glad hypocrite like us. Only failed ideals and wrong turnings will ever get you anywhere on earth or make anything with beauty or energy inside it. In the Bach F# Minor Fugue, or the slow C major tune in the Haydn sonata, the awful humming overwhelms the perfect technology, and everyone with ears tuned right is glad of it.

That hum is his ghost, still alive, but also it is the invisible audience sneezing and hacking; it is the ignorant applause after the wrong movement; it is pigeons in the rafters of the hall, cooing for bread; it is me blowing my nose and wiping my tears of joy in this music—in this odd, grand failure of a man.

Practicing the Blumenfeld Etude
for the Left Hand Alone

Forget, after a while, the right hand exists at all.
Whatever it's up to is no concern of yours,
whether pulling a trigger, counting change,
unfastening a dress. Maybe it's even
practicing yet another etude
for some silent interior piano. Meanwhile
your single sinister hand plays over and over
a stretch of notes, til even the fourth finger obeys,
wrist rotating on the pivot of the magisterial thumb,
an airplane doing show tricks in midair
banking this way and that to dazzle the crowd.
Such music your five fingers make!
The right hand is jealous now, an ignored
lover waiting for the phone to ring.

My Old Friend AT&T Writes Me
a Personal Letter

"Dear Mr. Holm,
Post office box one-eighty-seven may
be a terrific place to live, but for you—
it's more than just a home.
It's also a place to do serious business. . . ."
Dear Company,
How well you understand
my needs—my life—
how every night we light
tiny candles to dine
on a roast sparrow (nowhere
for leftovers, you know),
drink a small young burgundy
(no space here for wine to grow
old and big), then lie down
on our narrow bed for a little love.
Early in the morning
third-class mail tumbles
down the chute to drive us out
into the street. We only do
serious business here
when blizzards far away
stop the mail trucks or the master
takes a three-day holiday.
It would be nice to move.
Our place is a little cramped,
but we think your offer of
a "telecommunications program
designed exclusively to meet
the needs of people like me"
will make life better.
Please send more details
in a registered letter.
Maybe we should talk face-
to-face: our box or yours?

I notice you, like us,
live in a box, ten seventy-eight
in Duncansville, PA.
That's why you understand.
Sincerely, your old friend,
Mr. Holm.

Corporate Wind

The Company pays hard cash for all the wind
blowing over these bare hills near Dakota,
Chinook, Alberta Clipper, Tornado,
then raises up a thousand bone-white poles
topped with three blades to slice the air,
transform it into kilowatts of power.
Daily this must astonish the cows
who still graze on private grass below.
The Company says it owns this wind
in perpetuity or at least until
the glacier comes to collect the hills again.
In bright fall sun the blades all circle,
each in its own time, this way and that,
free-market wind still dancing its own dance.

Looking at God
for Bill "Cutz" Klas

"Drive eight miles west on Stampede Road. It's good gravel; when it dead-ends, you should see the mountain if it's out," say the locals.

"How will I know it?"

"If it's there, you'll know it."

I drive eight miles, past the In-His-Shadows Church, a wrecked pickup with a peace symbol dangling from a bent rearview mirror, a half-dozen cabins, up past heavy woods to high tundra, still snowless at the end of October, brown hummocks, red weeds, punctuated with an occasional mealy spruce. Eight-Mile Lake is half-frozen, dark blue polka-dotted with ice.

At the end of the road, there it is—two peaks, immense white shadows poking above the other ridges, bigger than anything ought to be at eighty miles' distance. The locals are right: if you can't tell you are in the presence of God when you see it, no one can explain it to you.

I remember an old friend in Minnesota who calls Lake Superior God, because it is always there—even when it is invisible, and you can't see across it when it isn't. Another might call the Grand Canyon God. They're all right. The point is: God is big— too big to miss, no matter how the human race wants to shrivel him down to size and buddy up. If you let God into your heart, he will explode it like a toy balloon. God is the heart—of the spacious firmament of all the circling galaxies.

I turn off the pickup and stand transfixed—listening. No wind, no motors, no birds, no talk, bright sun, maybe thirty degrees. The pickup pistons ping a little as they lose heat, then they fall silent too. It is the loudest silence I have ever heard, and it goes on for miles. Is this silence the noise of the mountain singing anthems to itself? Is it the noise of the joints inside the axis of the planet, rotating? Is the air praying? A half hour of this is enough—too much. I start the pickup and return downhill, every way you can go.

Denali, Alaska

Official Talk in Wuhan—1992

When nothing has happened there is no need
to mention it, it would only prove
embarrassing if certain policies
were brought up, though of course
everything, as you see, is fully
ordinary, moving forward, though without
any backward to move forward
from and everyone smiles and is
happy, doing their part, though of what
they are not too sure, only little
months and years have disappeared,
nothing much and nothing serious if
a little time goes quietly away
here and there, and isn't mentioned because
there's no need, really, besides what
good would it do anyone, it might
cause painful thoughts and you can
see for yourself clearly the shops
are full, there's plenty to eat, the future's
just around the corner, and the past
is looking better every day. Meanwhile
an old lizard the size of a bulldozer
perches on the flat cement roof.
All the sleepers in their cold flats
listen to his raspy breathing all night,
watch his scaly tail hang just over
the edge, wave back and forth past their window,
thud into the wall now and then
like a hanged body blown
against the gallows by the east wind.

Paul Wellstone—October 25, 2002

On a gray, sleety October day,
the plane goes down in the north woods
with the large-hearted senator
whose decency and respect for old ideals
made half the citizens almost happy
to be Americans in a dark time.
Down went his wife and his daughter too,
three campaign workers, two pilots,
eight in all, the radio says,
neglecting the ninth seat where Death
dressed in an ordinary suit
sat watching for his chance
to do a morning's harvesting.
Do you think he wasn't there
hitching a ride, invisible, just as
he sat in the box at Ford's Theatre,
held open the convertible door in Dallas?
He sits in the front seat of your car, too,
or waits feigning sleep with his head
resting on the next pillow in your bed.
So we go on to write the same poem,
sing the same sad song yet once more
not for the dead who have gone
over to the insensible kingdom
but for us who must now carry on
without them. This time, as so often
before, Death snatched a big one
when we could not stand to lose
his voice, which spoke, not alone,
but for us millions who longed
for a world green, alive, about to bloom.

Water Tango in the Sea of Cortez

for Julia and Marcy

Two women, one short, one tall,
stand in the sand to face the waves
as if the sea were their lover come
twice a day to tickle them.
They like this!, play coquette,
waiting for a swollen breaker
to soak them with spray, feigning
surprise, then dancing away just
slowly enough for foam to lick their toes.
The men who've lost interest in
dancing the tango with the surf
stand above the oncoming tide
to admire these women playing sea nymph.
They are jealous of the water.
One quotes Walt: "Dash me with amorous wet,"
while the women, disdaining literature,
continue being dashed, and liking it,
repaying the crooked fingers of the sea.

Coelacanth

In February, in tropical summer, we tour the marine museum in Tulear, west coast of Madagascar. It's a humid hundred inside and out. Even the bottles of formaldehyde sweat. Specimen after vinegary specimen of strange fish: "Endemique!" "Unique!" "Extinct!" Finally, the back room—what everyone comes to see after enduring the two hundred bottles of briny spines. The soft-spoken gold-skinned girl flips the fluorescent light, points— the pièce-de-résistance of fishdom: Coelacanth caught in the Mozambique Channel, the fish that should have been dead for seventy-five million years, that never evolved, that lives only in this hot and lonesome ocean east of Africa.

He floats in a long glass tank, facing us. Five feet of mud flaps, a shit-brown, bug-eyed lump, stumpy double fins, underslung jaw, spiny mess of a rudder. Was the carpenter of this Platonic form of ugliness drunk, dim witted, asleep at the helm of the ship of creation? This . . . this . . . this . . . How did this breathe . . . swim . . . survive . . . ? Was this too ugly even for the million sleek and ravenous Indian Ocean sharks to eat? Yet live it did, and does at this very moment, in the gray waters west of this room, this Quasimodo fish, this Phantom of Ichthyology, this ghost comrade of the pterodactyl.

Does Coelacanth broadcast news of what you looked like before you started your slow crawl out of the water, dropping your gills and your swim bladder in the tidal mud to stand upright in the sun, flexing your arrogant opposable thumbs?

Bend down now. Press your lips to the tank. Kiss the Coelacanth, offering praise and thanks that he became the fish of sorrows, the one who stayed behind to atone for your sins in his flesh. Whatever swims in the Indian Ocean swims inside you, too, the antique, useless parts, the old ugliness, the unevolved vitality that says: Stay alive! Stay alive! Stay alive!

A Visit with Fred Manfred's Ghost—
Blue Mounds, 1997

In this house cut into the red bluff,
a tall man sat in a low room
scribbling book after book after book.
When paper wearied of him, he rose up
from his chair and strolled to the hilltop.

On a July afternoon, pink wild roses,
yellow prickly pears, all in bloom,
cool north wind stirring the grass,
he stood on some red rock outcrop
surveying three states stretched out below
and thought this world a suitable home
for a tall man scribbling in a low room.

On another fine July afternoon
three years after neighbors claim he died,
I stroll up to admire the cactus blooming
but find him still there, standing on red quartz,
reciting a page or two of the big new book
that will finally open their eyes in New York.

His voice sounds like north wind through grass.
His gnarly finger, twice too long, points downhill
at a world that still looks suitable
for a tall man scribbling in a low room,
catching rides home on a slow billow of cloud.

John Clare's Last Letter

Browsing one day in the college library, I find on the shelf the letters of mad John Clare, a gay pink book. I wonder what old Clare said in his last letter after all those years in the loony bin? He wrote on March 8, 1860 to James Hipkins, an "unknown inquirer from the outside world." Clare was sixty-seven years old, twenty-three years locked up, four to go until the end. The editor says in his neat brackets, "This letter was [sent]." Most asylum letters never made it to the post. The letter says:

> Dear sir:
> I am in a Madhouse and quite forget your name or who you are you must excuse me for I have nothing to communicate or tell of and why I am shut up I don't know I have nothing to say so I conclude
> Yours respectfully,
> John Clare

Who was Hipkins? Why did he write? Had he fallen in love with those poems full of wrens, mice, badgers, larks, flies, crows, fish, snipes, owls, moles, and imaginary wives? Did he weep when Clare's little note came back to him in the "outside" world?

I leaf through the other last madhouse letters. Clare wrote to a son, long dead, inquiring if the boy ever saw his sister, even longer dead. Had life and death ceased to make any difference to him? Was that his madness—that he couldn't tell the difference between one world and the next, between the quick and the dead? Had the walls between worlds fallen down inside him, so that angels, devils, ghosts, specters, moved calmly back and forth between them?

The gay pink book falls open to the flyleaf. There's a name— Alec Bond—in neat red pen—long-dead Alec who loved mad John Clare and gay pink books and owls and badgers and even his old friend, me!

Those walls fall down inside me too, and I catch myself asking questions that will have to wait a long time to be answered.

Sometimes I think I'm shut up, too, and can't tell why and ought, respectfully, to conclude.

But sometimes, in empty libraries on muggy September days in Minnesota, the letters arrive with my name, written in a language I can read. News passes jauntily between worlds.

When this happens, what need does a man have to make anything up? The world is enough if you can say plainly what happens. If you say it plain enough, like mad John Clare, sometimes they shut you up, though what difference that makes no one can yet tell.

Wedding Poem

for Kristofer Dignus and Maria Heba, August 2000, Vík í Myrdal,
and for Schele and Phil, July 2002, Minneapolis

A marriage is risky business these days
Says some old and prudent voice inside.
We don't need twenty children anymore
To keep the family line alive,
Or gather up the hay before the rain.
No law demands respectability.
Love can arrive without certificate or cash.
History and experience both make clear
That men and women do not hear
The music of the world in the same key,
Rather rolling dissonances doomed to clash.

So what is left to justify a marriage?
Maybe only the hunch that half the world
Will ever be present in any room
With just a single pair of eyes to see it.
Whatever is invisible to one
Is to the other an enormous golden lion
Calm and sleeping in the easy chair.
After many years, if things go right,
Both lion and emptiness are always there;
The one never true without the other.

But the dark secret of the ones long married,
A pleasure never mentioned to the young,
Is the sweet heat made from two bodies in a bed
Curled together on a winter night,
The smell of the other always in the quilt,
The hand set quietly on the other's flank
That carries news from another world
Light-years away from the one inside
That you always thought you inhabited alone.
The heat in that hand could melt a stone.

A Note on the Door

One night I arrive at the door,
find a note: "I am sick.
Come in quietly." I don't need
to be told. The handwriting
gave me the news. While he aged
a month, it aged a century.

Now that hand wobbles
as if it walked the page
on a three-pronged cane
that can't find a safe spot
on the ice-covered index card.

I ask another doctor why
the hand gets news of death
long before the head. He
doesn't know, but knows
it's true. If the handwriting
firms up again, the patient
might live. If not . . .

Write a note on the margin
of this page. Look for signs:
a leaning *t,* a woozy *s,*
an *i* with curvature of the spine.

The Sanity of Denial

1

"Where we're going, there'll be wind, plenty of wind.
Best be prepared for anything." He says this
standing in his bathtub, held up by four arms;
weak legs wasted almost to bone wobble under him.
Two friends washed him to bring his fever down,
squeezing lukewarm water over what little meat
still sticks to his skeleton after fevers ate
their fill of liver, marrow, eyes, brain.
In the tub, he absently twirls his opal ring
twice too big for its finger, after these months
while exotic diseases washed over him,
tidal waves crashing into his body
one after another without relent: As soon as one
surge subsides, held back by passion and will,
another, more massive, smashes in. Under it all,
the black swell at the sea wall
loosened every foundation stone.

His bones told him the monkey virus
had tucked its napkin in and settled down
to eat long before his doctor's brain
that still kept faith with science and reason.

2

At the sea in Oregon we retreated
for a winter to listen to windblown tide
thump onto the rocks. In March,
the sky warmed, the sun beat back
the stubborn Pacific clouds, and three of us
climbed a little hill to an old lighthouse.
The warm grass astonished us, the new
yellow wildflowers tickled our bare feet.
We lay high above the noisy sea for hours,

the mammoth Victorian glass eye in the tower
turning and turning slowly above us.

We talked a little, praising the day, good luck,
good company, the sweetness of the world,
mostly silent as the sea winds
crawled slowly up the cliffs
to riffle the grass and cool our supine bodies.
To breathe, see, touch, listen, smell
on such an afternoon is enough.

Children arrived with noise, talk pilfered
from television, so we trudged back to the car.

What is there not to deny if this sweet world
were abruptly eaten out from under your own body,
leaving it falling into a black hole?
Who, in his right mind, would not say No!
shouting it into the gathering wind
with all the power left inside him?

Playing the Black Piano

One day when his eyes flicker with a little life, I go to the big
black Yamaha across from his hospital bed, the piano he bought
for friends and old age but, after the test, started practicing him-
self—slowly, methodically, badly, mathematical fingers playing
like a doctor, trying to get it exactly right, afraid he might lose
the patient with a wrong strike, unable ever to master forgetful-
ness: the necessary gift.

After two years, Bach's little minuet for Anna Magdalena
sounded like "The Parade of the Wooden Soldiers." After three
years, a piece finally came right. He called me thousands of miles
away one night, laid the phone on the black piano, and played the
first two pages of Beethoven's "Variations on Paisiello's *Nel Cor
Piu Non Mi Sento,*" a simple little tune over strummed chords,
and the first easy variations.

"Lovely," I said. "Now let's hear the rest of them."

"Don't be a smart ass," he said, "That's ten years' work." He
played it again on the phone, half a continent away, while I felt
in him the lineaments of gratified desire. There would be no ten
years, though nobody needed to say that during this moment of
spontaneous joy in the hands.

I take my own hands to the black piano, thinking this may be
the last music this lovely man hears in this world. Go out with
the best . . . I play a half-dozen preludes and fugues from *The
Well-Tempered Clavier,* Mozart's A Minor Rondo, "On Wings
of Song" transcribed by Liszt, "Jesu, Joy of Man's Desiring,"
"Scenes from Childhood." I improvise a little on "Tis the Gift
to Be Simple," then play some last Intermezzos of Brahms, full
of grief and singing in E major—slow waltzes out of a world no
one in their right mind wants to leave, no matter its misery and
stupidity. They all waltz inside me now: crippled Charlie and
my father dancing with Auntie Ole, my red-haired mother who
loved men so much, dancing with Michael and Alec, one on
each arm. Weeping solves nothing now, so I suck in my breath,
doing my best to make the black piano sing.

After Brahms, I think—what next?, begin browsing through

Beethoven. Here's his own copy: fingering and directions for these variations penciled in with circles above the *i* in his fussy hand, more used to prescriptions and lists than words like *dolce, espressivo, cantando, appassionato.* I play the variations carefully, as if they were a masterpiece. They are not. Only a lovely trifle, but this, too, like any small moment gives you the universe if you attend to it. At the end, I rise to go to his bed, not too sure he has heard anything at all. "And that, good doctor, is what it sounds like."

He opens his eyes. "Beautiful," he says, and does not call me a smart ass. After he goes, a day or two later, I find out he's willed me the black piano. I'm left to wonder: what music will it make now?

1700 36th Avenue

Your huge house was a curse.
Its many rooms allowed you
never to prune your life;
the house saved everything:
fifteen-year-old icebox notes
from your pilot lover: "Mike,
I'll make the cake tonight.
Get butter, Love Jimmy";
a beer coaster from Waterton,
Alberta, signed by John Allen
and twenty drunk roisterers;
a postcard from me with
a poem I'd forgotten writing;
a thousand negatives
for photos never again to be
developed on this planet;
an empty tin box with a note
from mother taped to the lid:
"These are your favorite
chocolate chips. Love . . ."
You must have thought,
like all of us, that if
these objects of your life
still lived in the back room,
you could visit them any time
you wanted, and then your life
would never disappear behind
you like a boat wake, yet
there you are in
a plastic bag on the fireplace
while we sit throwing, throwing,
telling stories, weeping,
imagining this big house
stripped, cleaned, Lysoled,
no dust or mildew left,
no pack-rat ghosts
to pace it in the dark.

Lemon Pie

For your last Thanksgiving in Minneota I invited half the
  universe,
Holm's single-handed feed-the-hungry, stuff-the-lonesome-
  stranger
with turkey and giblets and pie. Already death had winked at you
once or twice from behind its shadowy curtain.

My neighbors pitched in with gravy, bread, and labor. Thursday
  morning
Tom brought lemon pies, steaming, acid-sweet smell,
majestic meringues, soaring peaks of beaten egg white.
On the table cooling, you smelled them, found a fork,
and, a mischievous, sweet-toothed boy, were set to violate a hot
  meringue,
when I walked in and said, sharp of voice, "Get the hell out of
  there!
Those hot pies will be ruined if you dig into them."

"So what?" You shot me an insulted look. "They're only pies.
Eat them yourself." You skulked out into the morning. Toward
  night
your snit evaporated, and you resumed your usual grace and humor.
By then I'd grown my guilty conscience, remembering
that you lived under sentence of impending death.

I should have kept my mouth shut, one nagging inner voice
said to another, watched you put an entire hot lemon pie
into your gullet. What a hard business being human—
all we know and remember shadows every simple act.

The next Thanksgiving you lay close to death, all food
loathsome, indigestible. Kept half-alive with cans
of glutinous Ensure, we made a lemon pie to tempt you
into one more small pleasure, but you impaled
the pie with a fork, left it standing upright in the meringue,
and turned away, lost to all joy.

We are who we are until we aren't anything anymore but air.
I carry that steaming pie to my own grave, offering it to you
over and over again, atonement. I hear your wry voice
saying, as it said so often: "Eat dessert first; life is short and
   uncertain."

Lightning
for Phyllis Yoshida

You were a nervous man with a calm cat,
Lightning, whose attack mode
consisted of slowly raising one eyelid
or twitching a whisker as if it lived
in an atmosphere of pure molasses.
That cat respected gravity,
practiced only passive resistance to it.
An old friend who loathed cats, froze up
in their presence, liked him. He said,
"For a long time I thought he was stuffed;
then he shocked me and breathed."

Sometimes after a bourbon or two
you asked guests if they might enjoy
Lightning's new trick. You grabbed
torso and chest of sleeping Lightning,
held the tan, fat fluff ball overhead,
and waltzed and whirled through the kitchen
for maybe thirty seconds, stopped
and looked up while Lightning with
Republican deliberation stretched one
paw down, touched your forehead,
and held it there while we applauded.

O Lightning was a calm cat who had to be
startled into stretching. He slept at your feet
while you lay restless in your dying,
and then, like us, he outlived you a little while
but never did his trick again.

Beethoven in Victoria

Four Warsaw Poles and a Japanese woman pianist played
Beethoven's Wind Quintet last night in western Minnesota.
Outside, a February Alberta Clipper wind tried to bite every-
thing alive in the throat, thrashing it back and forth like the
stop sign on the state road.

On the way home, I held the car to its course, like a ship's
pilot in a gale, steering into the troughs of the swells. The high
beams lit up the frozen black furrows to port and starboard.
While the rondo still danced in my head, an obbligato to the
Clipper noise banging everything outside, I thought of you,
sailing on your boat, the *Cygnus,* the last time I heard this music.
Years ago we docked in Victoria harbor, marooned by a July
gale on the Straits of Juan de Fuca. What lovelier place to wait
out the wind with old friends? Julia and I strolled off to the gray
stone cathedral for a concert of festival music, a wind quintet,
with a piano, playing both Mozart's quintet and Beethoven's,
the loving godson's homage to that piece—his own quintet. The
stone vaulting of the old church carried the oboe and the clarinet
and all the rest up and over and down and around and over again.
The wind blew us into that music, so we gloried in it.

Meanwhile you and Don and J. R. had gone out to find the
gay bar listed in your guidebook, so Julia and I stopped for a
whiskey under a stuffed tiger in the Bengal Room at the Empress
Hotel, a grand Victorian stone homage to some antique imagina-
tion of empire. Thinking the three of you would be out til day-
light finding rowdy sexual adventures, we returned early down
the swaying dock to the boat, the parliament lights dancing a
jig in the black water. But there you all sat—drinking cocoa and
reading newspapers, listening to the scratchy nautical weather
report on the ship's radio like three old ladies after the quilting
bee. Not much gaiety in gay Victoria? I inquired disingenuously.
You said something sarcastic, then resumed the editorial page. I
whistled the Beethoven rondo and described two elderly English
ladies with sensible brown shoes gossiping in the pew in front
of us. Someone thought of spiking the cocoa with Bailey's. We

sat up late, laughing and happy, pleased with each other, the sea, and music.

Years later, I reinvent that night, reminded by Beethoven and this harsher wind; you are a few years dead before reaching fifty. But you are present, in my head, in this car, on a blustery night in Minnesota, almost palpable. We never touched; we were American men who admired one another, practiced mutual humor, generosity, consolation. I reach over to pat your invisible shoulder, then think: What is death anyway? You catch a newfangled disease that didn't even have a name when you got it, and it kills you. There is a hole in the sea where your boat sailed, and a hole in the table where your elbow rested next to a wine glass, and a hole in the middle of your black piano where the notes to Beethoven's rondo fit, and a hole in the lives of all of us on that boat that night.

Will imagination summon you back to the world of tacking and luffing and cocoa and remarks? You become the wind— coming and going as you please—invisible. If you think wind doesn't exist, watch the iron stop sign shimmy on its post; feel hair rise from your head; feel the bite on your face. Or listen for Beethoven's tune, disappeared for so many years into the calm air in the vaulting inside Victoria Cathedral on that balmy July night, blown back from Poland to Minnesota in cold February to sing again. Gone in the morning one more time, it will make its rounds after a while, like the wind and maybe like you, too, Camarado!

Magnificat

I have taken the text of "Magnificat" from the King James translation of the book of Luke 1: 46–55. The Walt Whitman lines interlaced with the "Magnificat" are from a poem first called in 1856 "Poem on the Proposition of Nakedness," afterward "Respondez!" and finally dropped from Leaves of Grass *in 1876. That was one of Whitman's worst editorial mistakes. The full text of the poem is worth finding by whatever title.*

Seattle, gray December;
rain slides off heavy madrona leaves;
the sky a giant battleship
anchored overhead.
In an elegant old house
on the eyebrow of a hill
a man lies close to death.
He recognizes no one anymore.
His friends wait in guest rooms
not daring to weep yet,
everyone's soul clotted
in a gray emulsion:
rage, grief, love,
nowhere to spend themselves.

A choir in town announces
the Bach *Magnificat* for Christmas.
"My soul doth magnify the Lord,
and my spirit rejoices." Maybe this music
will give me permission to grieve,
to magnify a little early.

Underage virgin and old lady,
Mary and Elizabeth,
both pregnant, both violating
custom, expectation, nature.
When they salute each other
babes leap in their wombs.
Unlikely.

The program says: the *Magnificat* celebrates
the way God turns the world upside down,
"reverses the ordinary,
disrupts the flow, inaugurates
surprising transformations."

In the elegant house on the eyebrow
of the hill, the young doctor
lies eaten at, insensible.
Is this God's work?
An old question,
it will not be answered.

The music begins. It curls, laves,
exalts, weeps, thumps, celebrates.
Every two minutes a new galaxy
dances through damp church air
into the ears, then the body—
ribbons of stars, garlands of planets,
space full of nothing but light.
It unlocks me and I weep,
whatever good that does.

Let every one answer! let those who sleep be waked! let none evade!
Must we still go on with our affections and sneaking?

He hath shewed strength with his arm; he hath scattered the proud in the
*   imagination of their hearts.*

Let that which stood in front go behind; and let that which was behind
*   advance to the front and speak;*

He hath put down the mighty from their seats, and exalted them of low
*   degree.*

Let men and women be mock'd with bodies and mock'd with Souls!
Let the love that waits in them, wait! let it die, or pass still-born to other spheres!
Let the people sprawl with yearning, aimless hands! let their tongues be broken! let their eyes be discouraged! let none descend into their hearts with the fresh lusciousness of love!

He hath filled the hungry with good things; and the rich he hath sent empty away.

Let churches accommodate serpents, vermin, and the corpses of those who have died of the most filthy of diseases!

For he hath regarded the low estate of his handmaiden: for, behold, from henceforth all generations shall call me blessed.

Let nothing remain but the ashes of teachers, artists, moralists, lawyers, and learn'd and polite persons!

He hath holpen his servant Israel, in remembrance of his mercy.

Let the world never appear to him or her for whom it was all made!
Let death be inaugurated!

Magnificat anima mea Dominum!

Let the limited years of life do nothing for the limitless years of death!
(What do you suppose death will do, then?)

Et exultavit spiritus meus in Deo salutari meo!

The music opens the flood tide
in me who is so sweetly alive!
but does nothing for the dying man.
He does not hear

196

even rain sliding
off madrona leaves.

Past all grief now,
he is about to disappear
into music, light, a bag of bone chips.
Soon we will neither
watch nor weep over him
but sing him back
from the world of light.

The singers bend over their music.
It's stern labor birthing beauty
from this printed page of old
chicken scratches and Latin prayers.
The cello saws; the trumpet
sucks heavy breath, wobbles, wets his lips,
hoping to spoil nothing.

It's a mystery why one
note following another
sometimes makes music,
sometimes breaks the heart,
sometimes not.

Don't ask the reason.

When we explain music
there'll be no need to die
or no need not to.

Listen as long as you can;
sing whenever the right tune
arrives inside you.

Buying a Stone in Echo, Minnesota

On a gray November day, almost snowing, two old friends drive
to the Echo Granite Works. Outside, a yard of broken stones;
half a name here, half a date there, a try at eternity that cracked
and went wrong. Inside, a dirt floor, an oil stove humming, a
pulley to lift the great dead weight up to carving height.

An old Norwegian comes up, says, "Can I help you with
something then?" What sort of help do you come for to the Echo
Granite Works?

"We want a black stone."

"Yah," he says and waits.

"For an old friend."

"Yah," he says, "Where?"

"Not in a graveyard."

"Where then?"

"In a garden."

"Black?" he says.

"Black."

"About this big?"

"That's about right."

"Smooth top or rough?" he asks. "Rough is cheaper."

"Rough." I suppose he has to ask these questions here in Echo.
It's colder inside the shack full of stones than outside in the north
wind.

"This black stone in a garden, . . ." he pulls at his pipe, digs
a pencil stub out of his pocket, "What should it say?"

Now there's a question. "It should say a name, two dates, both
known, and maybe a funny sentence."

"What's that?"

"Eat dessert first; life is short and uncertain."

He does not laugh. "One *s* or two in dessert then?"

"Go for two."

"That'll fit," he says.

What needs to be said will not fit on a black stone in a garden,
but none of us needs to say it; neither the two old friends nor the
Norwegian with the pencil stub printing careful letters on lined
paper, two precise *s*'s in dessert.

He says, "Too late this year. The ground'll be froze up soon."

Spring is better, we agree, for setting the black stone in the garden, after the mud dries up on the field road.

"Set her in concrete?" he asks.

"Just ground." We may have to move the black stone in the garden.

"That's about it then." He puts the pencil stub back, hands us the bill.

"The estate pays," we say, "for the black stone in the garden."

"Give me a call," he says, "after the frost goes."

Letting Go of What Cannot Be Held Back

Let go of the dead now.
The rope in the water,
the cleat on the cliff,
do them no good anymore.
Let them fall, sink, go away,
become invisible as they tried
so hard to do in their own dying.
We needed to bother them
with what we called help.
We were the needy ones.
The dying do their own work with
tidiness, just the right speed,
sometimes even a little
satisfaction. So quiet down.
Let them go. Practice
your own song. Now.

About the Author

Known and loved for his outspoken essays, his lively public talks and performances, his decades of service as a teacher—as well as for his keen and insightful wit, his enthusiastic love of art and music, and his fearless opinions—Bill Holm was an American original.

Born in Minneota, Minnesota, to the children of Icelandic immigrants, Holm embraced his small, rural hometown even as he waged a lifelong battle against provincialism, with the rich dynamics of this tension evident in such nonfiction books as *Eccentric Islands: Travels Real and Imaginary* and *The Heart Can Be Filled Anywhere on Earth: Minneota, Minnesota.*

He traveled widely, to Iceland on a Fulbright in 1979, as well as repeatedly in recent years to his summer home in Hofsós, which he wrote about in *The Windows of Brimnes: An American in Iceland*; and to China, where he taught on an academic exchange program in 1986 and again in 1992, as documented in *Coming Home Crazy: An Alphabet of China Essays.* Holm taught at Southwest Minnesota State University in Marshall from 1980 until he retired in 2007. In 2008 the McKnight Foundation bestowed their eleventh annual Distinguished Artist Award upon him.

From the very beginning of his writing career, Holm made his reputation as poet as well as an essayist, publishing his first book of poetry, *Boxelder Bug Variations,* in 1985 along with his first book of prose, *The Music of Failure. The Dead Get By with Everything,* his second book of poetry, came out in 1991, and his third poetry title, *Playing the Black Piano,* in 2004.

Upon Holm's untimely death at age 65 in 2009 from septic pneumonia, Garrison Keillor said, "Bill Holm was a great man and unlike most great men he really looked like one. Six-foot-eight, big frame, and a big white beard and a shock of white hair, a booming voice, so he loomed over you like a prophet and a preacher, which is what he was. I wish I'd been there to catch him as he fell. I hope his Icelandic ancestors are waiting to welcome him to their rocky corner of heaven. I hope his piano goes to someone who will love it as much as he did. I hope that people all across Minnesota will pick up one of his books and see what the man had to say."

More Books from Milkweed Editions

To order books or for more information,
contact Milkweed at (800) 520-6455
or visit our Web site (www.milkweed.org).

**Willow Room, Green Door:
New and Selected Poems**
Deborah Keenan

**With Mouths Open Wide:
New and Selected Poems**
John Caddy

**Black Dog, Black Night:
Contemporary Vietnamese Poetry**
Nguyen Do and Paul Hoover, Editors and Translators

**River of Words:
Young Poets and Artists on the Nature of Things**
Pamela Michael, editor

Milkweed Editions

Founded in 1979, Milkweed Editions is one of the largest independent, nonprofit literary publishers in the United States. Milkweed publishes with the intention of making a humane impact on society, in the belief that good writing can transform the human heart and spirit.

Join Us

Milkweed depends on the generosity of foundations and individuals like you, in addition to the sales of its books. In an increasingly consolidated and bottom-line-driven publishing world, your support allows us to select and publish books on the basis of their literary quality and the depth of their message. Please visit our Web site (www.milkweed.org) or contact us at (800) 520-6455 to learn more about our donor program.

Milkweed Editions, a nonprofit publisher, gratefully acknowledges a grant from the McKnight Foundation to support the publication of *The Chain Letter of the Soul: New and Selected Poems,* by Bill Holm. In 2008, the Foundation recognized Bill Holm with the McKnight Distinguished Artist Award, an acknowledgement of his positive impact on the quality of our state's cultural life over more than three decades. The Foundation is pleased to play a role in this continued celebration of Bill's life, his artistic passion, and his many contributions to the arts in Minnesota.

THE MᶜKNIGHT FOUNDATION

Milkweed Editions also gratefully acknowledges sustaining support from Anonymous; Emilie and Henry Buchwald; the Patrick and Aimee Butler Family Foundation; the Dougherty Family Foundation; the Ecolab Foundation; the General Mills Foundation; the Claire Giannini Fund; John and Joanne Gordon; William and Jeanne Grandy; the Jerome Foundation; Constance and Daniel Kunin; the Lerner Foundation; Sanders and Tasha Marvin; the McKnight Foundation; Mid-Continent Engineering; the Minnesota State Arts Board, through an appropriation by the Minnesota State Legislature, a grant from the Wells Fargo Foundation Minnesota, and a grant from the National Endowment for the Arts; Kelly Morrison and John Willoughby; the National Endowment for the Arts; the Navarre Corporation; Ann and Doug Ness; Ellen Sturgis; the Target Foundation; the James R. Thorpe Foundation; the Travelers Foundation; Moira and John Turner; Joanne and Phil Von Blon; Kathleen and Bill Wanner; and the W. M. Foundation.

MINNESOTA STATE ARTS BOARD

NATIONAL ENDOWMENT FOR THE ARTS
A great nation deserves great art.

TARGET.

Interior design by Rachel Holscher, Bookmobile
Typeset in Bembo
by Kim Doughty, Bookmobile
Printed on acid-free Glatfelter paper
by Friesens Corporation